MY VOICE, HIS HEART

Experiencing Prayer in God's Will

MY VOICE, HIS HEART

Experiencing Prayer in God's Will

A six week journey with a personal prayer coach

CATHY ENDEBROCK

Tranquility Press 2021

Copyright © 2021 Cathy Endebrock

All rights reserved. No part of this book may be copied, displayed, or distributed without prior written permission.

For information:
Tranquility Press
723 W University Ave #300-234
Georgetown TX 78626
https://www.tranquilitypress.com/
tranquilitypress@gmail.com

Unless otherwise indicated, Scripture quotations are from the Holy Bible, English Standard Version (ESV), copyright 2001 by Crossway.

Audio downloads copyright Let's Pray Today, LLC. Used with permission.

Cover design and artwork: Suzi Kramer

ISBN: 978-1-950481-30-9

Library of Congress Control Number: 2021935175

Library of Congress Cataloging-in-Publication Data
Names: Endebrock, Cathy, 1970- author.
Title: My voice, his heart : experiencing prayer in god's will : six weeks with a personal prayer coach
Description: Georgetown, Texas : Tranquility Press, 2021
Identifier: LCCN: 2021935175 | ISBN 978-1-950481-30-9 (paperback)
Subjects: LCSH: Christian women—Religious life | Prayer—Christianity
Classification: LCC BV4527 | DDC 248.3/2082—dc23

TO MY GREAT-GRANDMOTHER

whose spoken prayers surrounded me each night as I drifted off to sleep in the bedroom across the hall. Hearing my name carried to the King's throne in the dark hours set my young heart and mind aright. Your prayers inspire and surround me still.

TABLE OF CONTENTS

About the Author..9
A Note from Cathy..11
Helpful Information...13

Week 1: Introduction to Prayer...16
Day 1: Let's Speak Openly, Shall We?..................................19
Day 2: Let's Get on the Same Page......................................23
Day 3: Ready. Set. Pray...29
Day 4: A Bike for You to Ride...33
Day 5: An Intimate Conversation..39

Week 2: Adoration..44
Day 1: Infinite, All Powerful, Ever Present...God................47
Day 2: Prayer Perfection..53
Day 3: Perfect Posture..59
Day 4: The Heart of the Matter...65
Day 5: A Holy Hug...71

Week 3: Confession..76
Day 1: Sweet Confessions..79
Day 2: Confession & Repentance...85
Day 3: The Truth God Reveals..91
Day 4: Turning Toward Love: Understanding Sacrifice.......97
Day 5: Nothing Is Better than God......................................105

Week 4: Thanksgiving..108
Day 1: The Pessimist, the Optimist, and the Psalmist........111
Day 2: What Is Thankfulness?..117
Day 3: The Favor of a King...123
Day 4: Thanksgiving for Provision, Favor, and Blessing.....129
Day 5: The Sacrifice of Thanksgiving..................................135

Week 5: Supplication..140
Day 1: Suppli-What?..143
Day 2: The Obvious Truth..149
Day 3: Asking with His Word..153
Day 4: Asking Big for Another..159
Day 5: Deep Desires...163

Week 6: Listening..170
Day 1: Ready. Set. Listen...173
Day 2: Desire to Hear...179
Day 3: Seek to Understand...185
Day 4: Recognizing God's Voice....................................193
Day 5: Awake and Aware..201

Appendix...206
Leader's Guide..209
Answers to Weekly Exercises..211
Bible Basics, Translations, & Selecting a Bible.................230
Prayer Styles and Formats..234

Endnotes 239
Connecting to Prayer Groups...244
Favorite Books on Prayer..245
Acknowledgements...246
Other Resources from Cathy Endebrock.........................247

ABOUT THE AUTHOR

Cathy Endebrock has been coaching and ministering to women for over 25 years as a radio host, women's ministry director, author, and through her non-profit, "Let's Pray Today Ministries." One of her greatest joys is seeing women embrace an intimate and transformative relationship with Jesus Christ through prayer and Bible study. Her ministry's series of prayer CDs and MP3s have been endorsed by Kay Arthur, founder of Precept Ministries, and Tim Clinton, president of the American Association of Christian Counselors.

As an ambitious young woman, Cathy believed a life of international travel and career success was the ultimate joy and goal, but found that life lacking. She became overwhelmed with the desire to know God deeply and personally, jumped into the deep waters of prayer, and discovered the greatest joy and adventure of her life: Jesus.

As a Christian talk show host, Cathy has interviewed political figures, musicians, national ministry leaders, and up-and-coming youth leaders. "Sometimes we simply need a word of encouragement, a shift in perspective, or a moment of truth to awaken us to the call. My hope is to affect that in our audience and in the women I am blessed to serve."

Cathy has been married to Eric, her high school sweetheart, for over 27 years. They have three daughters: Aliya, Jordan, and Faith.

"My Voice, HIS Heart" coached Bible study is the most recent culmination of Cathy's passion for prayer. She merges her direct but fun-loving style, excitement for scripture, and desire to help others experience God deeply and intimately.

A NOTE FROM CATHY

WELCOME, FRIEND.

Today, we begin moving together toward a deeper relationship with God through prayer. We will begin leaning into the God Who created us with gentle, knowing hands and life-giving breath. As He draws near to us, we will learn how to find our words, speak our hearts to Him, and listen. We will discover together that nothing in this world or in this life can come close to lifting our spirits, calming our hearts, or healing our hurts like time spent in the presence of our Creator. God loves you more than you can imagine.

I am not going to spend time showing you the hundreds of places in scripture that convince us that we ought to pray—I believe if you are holding this book in your hands, you do not need convincing. Instead, we will begin our actual prayer journey. We will pray for you as you grow in your relationship with God. We will find ways to pray that most suit how God has designed you. Prayer is not established around a rigid set of rules. It is a living, breathing, engaged relationship that is unique to each child of God. We will explore together different ways, times, and approaches of prayer—not by merely reading about it but by practicing it. Why? Because prayer touches every aspect of your life more than you can imagine.

This is not just another book about prayer. The goal of our time together is not simply for you to know more about prayer. Knowledge abounds in the world today, and most are no closer to God for it. The goal instead is for you to know God personally and intimately through prayer. At the end of our six weeks together, you will have spent six weeks actively praying, engaged in relationship with God—seeking, speaking, listening, and loving. Why? Because time with God changes you more than you can imagine.

Thank you for committing this time. My commitment to you is that I will be the best coach I know how to be. I will share everything I am able with the words and time I have, and I will encourage you each step of the way, holding you accountable to your commitment until the very end of our journey together.

MY VOICE, HIS HEART

May the thoughts and concepts shared in this short book be received with the power, purpose and love I intended when I began to put pen to paper. As we pursue Him together, may He transform us more than we could ever know or dream to be possible.

May God richly bless every moment we are together—pressed down, shaken together and running over,

Cathy

HELPFUL INFORMATION

OPTION OF PRAYER DOWNLOADS

This engaged prayer study is designed to either stand on its own, or work alongside the "Prayer for Beginners" downloadable audio mp3 or CD. If you are doing this study as part of a group, you have likely already decided whether or not you will use the supplemental material. If you are doing this as an independent study and you would like the additional company of a virtual prayer partner, you can download the mp3 at no additional cost by going to www.letspraytoday.com/HisHeart. Whichever you choose, this is tailored for you; there is no wrong approach here.

SUGGESTIONS FOR STUDY

Each day we will spend 15–20 minutes in study and prayer. I want this to be manageable for you. We will stay focused so you can have time alone with God each day. I have primarily used an ESV (word for word) Bible translation, and indicated wherever another translation is used. If you use a different Bible translation, that is fine. All answers to daily exercises can be found in the Appendix. If you do not have a Bible, there is a section in the Appendix ("Bible Basics, Translations & Selecting a Bible") to help you select a Bible that will be special for you moving forward.

Follow these steps to maximize your time and success in these next six weeks:

1. Find a comfortable place in your home that affords you some privacy and quiet. Keep a Bible, this workbook, a few highlighters or colored pencils, and a journal near this location for easy access.

2. Select a time each day to complete our time together and schedule it on your phone with a fun, cheery 15-minute alert.

3. When the alert sounds, turn on your favorite worship station or playlist while you wrap up whatever you are doing.

4. Stop busy work when it is time. Dishes, housework, homework, projects, or whatever other incomplete tasks are waiting for you can simply wait another 15-20 minutes. Remember your commitment. You have given God your "Yes" and His heart is ardent to receive your voice in His throne room.

5. Put your phone on silent. Turn off the music. Smile. Say "Thank You, LORD." Enjoy your appointed time with Him.

SHARING THIS STUDY - LEADER'S GUIDE

Once you complete this study, consider going through it a second time with a group of friends. You do not need to consider yourself a leader if that makes you tremble in the knees. You are simply a woman who loves Jesus and wants to share His love with others.

If you are guiding other women through this study, thank you and may God bless you abundantly for your commitment. There is a brief Leader's Guide in the Appendix to help with some ideas for discussion preparation and managing group dynamics.

Prayer should not be regarded as a duty which must be performed, but rather as a privilege to be enjoyed, a rare delight that is always revealing some new beauty.
E.M. BOUNDS

The world has yet to see a Christlike, victorious, fruitful believer who was not a person of considerable prayer.
JIM CYMBALA

Week One

WEEK 1: INTRODUCTION TO PRAYER, DAY

DAY 1

Week 1: Introduction to Prayer

"Dear God in heaven Who loves me more than I can imagine, I turn to You and draw near to You with a sincere heart filled with hope. I am Your daughter who loves You and desires to know You more. Please forgive me for failing to seek after You as my greatest love. I have looked to the world instead of to You to find joy and fulfillment. Thank You for Your mercy and the grace that draws me back and tethers my heart to Yours. Thank You for Your promise to draw near to me as I draw near to You. Teach me to pray as I go day by day in this study. In Jesus' name, amen."[1]

LET'S SPEAK OPENLY, SHALL WE?

There is something about the spoken word that carries power and clarity and connects us to others. When we consider prayer, however, we inherently understand that we are dealing with something personal and intimate, and understandably we might immediately think of silent prayer. We have plenty of examples in God's Word where leaders, prophets, disciples, and Jesus Himself prayed silently. However, the overwhelming occurrences of prayer in the Bible are audible, spoken prayer. During my years as a Women's Ministry Director for my church and in other leadership roles, I have found that while most ladies would feel a reasonable level of comfort with silent prayer, the large majority would become quite undone with the idea of spoken prayer. Yet spoken prayer comes with an immediate corporate connection that silent prayer does not. We want to focus our efforts where we can experience the greatest level of growth and have the deepest degree of impact. For these two reasons we will be spending our time together engaging in spoken prayer. Take courage; great growth often comes from great challenge.

If you already have an established prayer time, when you go into your "prayer closet" or other quiet place to spend time alone in prayer, that is wonderful. We are going to build on this foundation by beginning to give our voice to the cries of our heart in prayer as much as we are able. There are certainly some things we may not have the words to express and that is okay. We will begin using our voice in prayer privately so we can get more comfortable with using our voice in prayer with others.

I have been asked which is more important: 1) praying privately to the Father where no man can see; 2) praying corporately together as the people of God; or 3) praying publicly in ministry to others. This is an excellent question and one that places us with the top religious scholars of Jesus' day. In Matthew 22:34-40 we see experts in the law posing what they deemed to be the single most difficult question to be answered: of all the commands, which is the most important? Without skipping a beat, Jesus replied, "Love the Lord your God with all your heart, with all your soul, and with all your mind…[and] love your neighbor as yourself."

We can apply Jesus' response to our query. Which type of prayer is most important? It is the prayer that at each individual moment will let us accomplish loving God, loving self, and loving others. Jesus joyfully hands us the assignment to take everything He has taught us and go out and love others.[2] If we are not spending time alone with God in prayer privately, we will have little power as we go to pray with others corporately and publicly. Likewise, if we are too timid to go out and pray with others corporately and publicly, what is that telling us about our love for God? Are we loving Him with all our heart, soul, and mind if we are refusing to do the one thing He has told us He will equip us to do?

Please hear me. I am not saying the goal of prayer is ministry. We are not spending six weeks together so you can go do something I want you to do. That is not my place. The goal of prayer is relationship. My charge and commitment is to help you grow in relationship with our Heavenly Father in prayer. In these six weeks you will discover and develop your uniquely beautiful and powerful voice in prayer. He will be the One who prompts you to apply what He has given you.

One final note: When we are discussing our voice in prayer, I am not referring to speaking in tongues. There are many books on the subject, but this is not one of them. I have addressed this type of prayer in the Appendix under "Prayer Styles & Formats."

WEEK 1: INTRODUCTION TO PRAYER, DAY 1

Please know that I understand spoken prayer is going to require more energy, substantially more focus, and at times more courage than you may feel you have. God promises that He will not only reward your efforts in prayer,[3] but He will also provide the strength, insight, and courage when you do not have it on your own.[4] You. Can. Do. This.

What do you believe you will require more of to engage in spoken prayer? (Check all that apply.)

☐ Energy   ☐ Courage   ☐ Focus   ☐ Confidence

☐ Insight   ☐ Trust   ☐ _____   ☐ Yes, please...all

Let me assure you, you are not going to be asked to stand in front of an audience and lead in prayer. If that request ever comes, it will not be from me but from God—and He will equip you for it.

Let's get personal and compare the difference between silent prayer and spoken prayer. Go back to today's opening prayer. I'm guessing that as you began today, you either read the text matter-of-factly or you prayed through it silently. In a moment we're going to go back and give voice to our prayer. I would like you to briefly prepare for prayer. Breathe deeply and slowly exhale. Feel the tension leaving your shoulders. Breathe in deeply again, and as you breathe out gently, allow your body and mind to feel the peace your relationship with God brings. Now go back and voice today's opening prayer directly before our loving Father, adding in at the end your own words of request for the personal needs you marked above.

How was voicing the prayer different from silently reading it?

_____

_____

_____

_____

MY VOICE, HIS HEART

Did taking a moment to stop and prepare for prayer make a difference for you? If so, how?

_____

_____

_____

_____

If you felt a little unusual voicing this prayer out loud and putting in words of your own, hang in there—it gets easier. I'm proud of you for persevering in this. More importantly, God's heart is swelling over you and your courageous commitment to Him.

Breathe deeply, relax your shoulders, gentle your thoughts, and enjoy closing today's study with a few words of prayer.

"Thank You, Lord, for teaching me today. Thank You for leading me here and drawing close. I need You and I love You. Thank You for loving me with Your powerful, life-changing love. Keep my ear attentive to Your still, small voice as I walk in the light of Your love today. In Jesus' name, amen."[5]

WEEK 1: INTRODUCTION TO PRAYER, DAY

DAY 2

Week 1: Introduction to Prayer

"Heavenly Father, You alone have set the time and season for everything. You have established Your will and purposed my life for good. Thank You for the grace You extend to me every day. Help me to extend that same grace to others. As I grow in relationship with You, help me to also grow in relationship with others. In Jesus' name, amen."[6]

LET'S GET ON THE SAME PAGE

- Everyone is supposed to pray—or are they?
- We know exactly what is and isn't considered prayer—or do we?
- We can generally observe someone for a fairly brief period of time and know whether or not s/he is praying—or can we?
- Effective prayer will always include a sense of God's presence—or will it?

We all have different ideas and beliefs about prayer. Let's evaluate our varied views so we can get on the same page and know what exactly we are talking about.

I'm going to ask you to take 10 minutes to complete a true-or-false Review of Prayer. I really want us to <u>not</u> go back and erase answers but to be able to take a close look and remember where our own perceptions and tendencies exist. If you have a challenging time with the true or false claim of the statement, consider it from the perspective of a general, firm statement without caveats attached—that is, whether the statement is 100% true.

These are all statements I have struggled with and worked through personally or with other women. Don't worry if you find yourself on the fence with some of these. If you are doing this study as part of a group, you can have some fun discussion time when everyone is done completing the review on their own. When we are done with the review, you will find what I believe scripture supports as the most accurate evaluation of each statement. *We may disagree and that is okay.* Our prayers will not be any less effective because two sisters in Christ have different perspectives on scripture. Quite the opposite; we thank God for our different perspectives because they spur us on to deeper study and enable us to have conversations about His Word. That will put a smile on His holy face every day of the week! It's important to me to know what my teachers and coaches believe and why, and I want to make sure you are given that same opportunity as we grow together in prayer.

MY VOICE, HIS HEART:
TRUE & FALSE PRAYER REVIEW

1.	T	F	Some people do not have the gift of prayer.
2.	T	F	A good Christian must pray every day.
3.	T	F	In order to pray effectively we must bow our head and be on our knees with our hands together.
4.	T	F	If we pray throughout the day as we go, concerted daily prayer becomes less important.
5.	T	F	We should not pray when we are angry; we should wait until we have calmed down.
6.	T	F	If we do not sense God's presence when we are praying, we are likely out of touch with God and He is not listening.
7.	T	F	The reason we should always pray is because we are commanded to by God.
8.	T	F	We must pray only to God the Father and not to Christ Jesus the Son; Jesus prays for us, we are not supposed to pray to Him.
9.	T	F	Prayer is designed by God to be easy and only less mature Christians really have to work at it.
10.	T	F	Prayer is about lifting our requests to God and making our needs known to Him; it is separate from our relationship with Him.
11.	T	F	The more God loves you, the more He will answer your prayer.
12.	T	F	Morning prayer is far more effective than bedtime or evening prayer.

MY VOICE, HIS HEART

Well done! I wish I could see your responses and hear your thoughts on these statements.

- Circle the number of each statement that was difficult to answer.

- Highlight every statement you marked as true. List the corresponding numbers for each of those true statements here:

_____

In the Appendix (p. 211) is a section titled "My Voice, His Heart: True & False Prayer Review" that goes through each statement and provides scripture and explanation as to why every statement is *false*. Please look up the corresponding explanation for every statement you marked as true.

What misconceptions surprised you or caused you to stop and think about where they came from?

_____

_____

_____

_____

As I was preparing to speak at a prayer conference in Austin, Texas, I began working through all the different approaches to prayer, recognizing that some beliefs, practices, and customs had become so ingrained among different individuals, groups, and cultures that prayer was no longer considered genuine if certain rules were not followed, if specific words were not used, or if special criteria were not met. *Prayer,* in some instances, has wrongly become a measuring rod for how spiritual a person is or is not.

The assessment you just completed is similar to the one I designed for that particular prayer conference. We ended up with a white board full of additional misconceptions on prayer that various attendees had picked up

WEEK 1: INTRODUCTION TO PRAYER, DAY 2

over the years. There was a lot of laughter and many learning moments. We let ourselves off the hook that day for falling short and not living up to some perfect Christian standard. Let's let ourselves off the hook and enjoy this journey. Let's commit to pursuing an intimate, loving relationship with God and take our focus off of ticking any boxes or doing or saying something in prayer the "right" way.

What other misconceptions have you learned about prayer that you have had to unlearn or get past in order to enjoy time in prayer?

_____

_____

_____

I hope you are willing to share what you are writing down here with others if you are in a group. I wish I could be in the room to discuss them with you. I imagine some past beliefs may even sound a bit silly to us now.

CLOSING PRAYER

Breathe, relax your shoulders, and enjoy a moment of prayer as you wrap up today's study. Before you close with your "amen," add in a few words of your own, either thanking God for something He has revealed to you or seeking His help with an unexpected hardship.

"Father in heaven Who loves me and delights in me, I want to know You more, love You more, and live a life in relationship with You. Thank You, loving Father, for the mind, heart, body, and spirit You have given me. Use them all for Your glory according to Your good will, Your beautiful purpose, and Your unfailing love.
[*Private words here.*]
In Jesus' name, amen."[7]

WEEK 1: INTRODUCTION TO PRAYER, DAY

DAY 3

Week 1: Introduction to Prayer

"I come before you today, Heavenly Father, ready for the day You have made. I rejoice and my heart is glad. You are my Father and I am Your child. You delight in me. Help me to understand that I do not have to work to earn Your great love—You give it freely. Thank You for Your forgiveness and grace. Open my eyes to Your truth and align my will to Yours, that I would see clearly, understand rightly, and love deeply. In Jesus' name, amen."[8]

READY. SET. PRAY.

I want to tell you again how I admire your commitment to pursuing a deeper relationship with God in prayer. I know so much pulls at our time and calls for our attention. Many times I have found myself saying, "If only I had more time, I would be able to pray more like I desire;" or, "I need to join a prayer group once I finish this project;" or, "If only my husband would join me, I would pray more often;" or a host of other wishful thoughts that made me feel hopeful and assured me of my value and commitment to prayer, without actually spending time in prayer.

When I was asked to write a Bible study on prayer to tie in with our ministry's Prayer for Beginners audio recording, in my spirit I said, "Yes, LORD, if You will confirm this is what You would have me do, I will do it!" Yet after twelve months of encouragement in prayer, getting a resounding "Yes" from my board of directors, and even getting a check in the mail to cover the cost of publication, I kept allowing my days to fill up—week after week and month after month, even to the point of finding other things to do every time I sat in front of the computer to begin working on the study.

I was excited about writing the study. I had notes everywhere of what I wanted to share and the scriptures I would use. I envisioned the women who would be my new friends even though I might never meet them face to face. My wishful thoughts assured me of my value and commitment to writing this study; yet it was still not getting written. Wishful thoughts are

MY VOICE, HIS HEART

certainly better than dismissive thoughts, or no thoughts, but they are still only thoughts. Without action they accomplish nothing. After twelve months of wishful thinking and good intentions, this study remained unwritten and benefitting no one.

Can you relate? Have you been wanting to engage more deeply in prayer, but never seem to have the time? Is there a project or request you have committed to before God but weeks, months, or years continue to pass with no progress?

Would you be willing to share your heart with me here? Would you write down your hopes for your prayer life, your desires for a deeper relationship, or a "yes" that you have given God but have yet to make progress on?

_____

_____

_____

_____

_____

God shared a short story in His Word that has completely changed how I respond in my commitment to Him—and especially how I prioritize prayer. In a parable in Matthew 21:28-32, Jesus contrasts the opposing responses and actions of two sons:

> *"What do you think? There was a man who had two sons. He went to the first and said, 'Son, go and work today in the vineyard.'*
> *'I will not,' he answered, but later he changed his mind and went.*
> *Then the father went to the other son and said the same thing. He answered, 'I will, sir,' but he did not go.*
> *Which of the two did what his father wanted?"*
> *"The first,"* they answered.

WEEK 1: INTRODUCTION TO PRAYER, DAY 3

With whom do you most identify?

☐ The first son　　　　　　☐ The second son

When God showed me this scripture, I kicked up a fuss at first but then I owned it. Yes, I was certainly the second son. I had placated and justified myself with all my wishful thoughts of what my prayer life would look like once I "had the time" or "joined that group." Surely all my intentions firmly established that I valued prayer, right? After all, who in their right mind would commit to writing a study on prayer if God wasn't her top priority? God was gentle with me. He showed me that a "yes" is not enough. Wishful thinking was easy and made me feel good, but it is the follow-through that God wants.

What about you? Are you ready to pursue a relationship with God as a real priority by following through on your "Yes" to Him?

☐ I am ready to do this. Let's go!

☐ Wishful thinking and happy thoughts are my comfort zone. I'm anxious about stepping forward.

☐ I don't feel ready, but I'm trusting God to help me.

God accepts us where we are. He will be our Helper and Guide as we step forward in relationship with Him.

INTERACTIVE PRAYER DOWNLOAD

If you are using the Let's Pray Today Ministries "Prayer for Beginners" mp3 download, go to the Introduction, on Track 1, and listen all the way through to the end of the Introduction (approx. 7 minutes). You may use the closing prayer of the introduction as your closing prayer for today, rather than the concluding prayer provided below, or you can pray through both. Your choice, friend.

In closing today's time, share with God those thoughts you recorded concerning your hopes and desires—and possibly that 'yes' you gave but have yet to follow through on.

MY VOICE, HIS HEART

CLOSING PRAYER

"Heavenly Father, above all things You desire a relationship with me. Forgive me for saying 'Yes' to that relationship but failing to follow through in pursuing time with You in prayer. Help me to not be satisfied with wishful thinking but to be satisfied only by real time with You. You say in Psalm 37:4 that You will give me the desires of my heart.

I bring You my desire and hope of [*private words here*].

I ask for Your help, strength, and awareness in following through on my 'Yes' to You. Thank You for being with me. Thank You for loving me. In Jesus name, amen."[9]

WEEK 1: INTRODUCTION TO PRAYER, DAY

DAY 4

Week 1: Introduction to Prayer

"Heavenly Father, You have fashioned me in Your own likeness. You have made me valuable; You have made me capable; You have made me belong. I am never alone because You are with me always. Live and love through me today with everyone You bring my way. In Jesus' name I pray. Amen."[10]

A BIKE FOR YOU TO RIDE

Do you remember your first bike? Mine had a white banana seat and the tallest, narrowest, U-shaped handlebar ever. I could fit two friends behind me but not even an eight-year-old had a small enough backside to fit on that handlebar. There is nothing like a bike to bring a child a sense of freedom and joy. We are willing to go through the pain of scraped knees, the fear of falling, and the wobbly unbalance because of the exhilaration that awaits us on the other side.

Let's Pray Today Ministries has a slogan: "Prayer is like riding a bicycle. You can read about it, you can learn about it, you can even watch others do it—but until you do it yourself, you're missing the best part!" The freedom, joy, and exhilaration of prayer is even better than that bike we dearly loved. It is worth the wobbly unbalance, fear, and pain of shifted priorities.

Just as there are countless types of bicycles one can choose to ride, there are countless ways to pray: different formats, structures, models, styles, degrees of formality…I've read more books on prayer than I have read on any other single topic. I encourage you to read books on prayer and gain all the insight you can; but never, ever allow learning *about* to prayer to replace *engaging in* actual prayer. Been there, done that, wrote a study so you won't do the same. When we settle for knowledge at the expense of relationship, we're no better than off than those who live in the dark without the light to help them.

MY VOICE, HIS HEART

Have you ever allowed learning about prayer to replace actually engaging in prayer?

☐ Nope.   ☐ Who, me? Um...   ☐ Yep, that would be me.

Let's commit together to never allow knowledge of God or knowledge of prayer to replace an actual relationship with God and intimate time in prayer. If you will commit to this with me, please sign your name next to mine:

_____   *Cathy Endebrock*

For this Bible study, I have chosen to align with the ACTS prayer model because it is super easy to understand, follow, and remember. This is the same format used in the downloadable MP3s you may be including, so it ties in well if you're using both. *ACTS* is an acrostic for Adoration, Confession, Thanksgiving, and Supplication. Weeks 2-6 of this study will walk through each element. The ACTS structure works well for silent, voiced, meditative, private, partner, and group prayers.

In the Appendix you'll find a list of my favorite books on prayer, as well as different structures and formats of prayer you might try in the future. I will mention here one of my favorite types of prayer that is easy, fun, and dear to my heart: Popcorn Prayer.

It is special to me because it was the type of prayer I was engaged in when I first felt the powerful presence of the Holy Spirit in group prayer. Until then, I had believed that the most powerful presence of the Holy Spirit in groups was only experienced in times of song-based worship. Was I ever wrong. The Popcorn Prayer format is perfect for beginners, and a new way to approach group prayer for long-time prayer warriors. You can download instructions for Popcorn Prayer from the Let's Pray Today website (LetsPrayToday.com/HisHeart) if you want to invite a group of friends together for a fun and spiritually uplifting time. Can anyone say, "Prayer Party?"

Having said all this, please know that you do not need any special format, style, or structure for prayer to be effective. These are all simply starting points to help organize our thoughts and time in prayer. As you grow in

WEEK 1: INTRODUCTION TO PRAYER, DAY 4

prayer, you'll develop a deeper relationship with God and begin to find your own voice. It's likely you will cease using any special format at all.

THREE MINUTES AT THE START TO SET THE DAY APART

Multiple research studies have been done on the importance of how we spend the first few minutes of each day. Like the coin dropped into the vending machine, our selection will determine what we snack on. Imagine if that same selection dropped every hour for the next eight hours for your consumption. You might rethink your choice on how you invested that initial coin. Research has shown that as brief as the first three minutes of our day are, they actually continue to impact our frame of mind, mood, productivity, emotions, and perceptions for the next eight hours of the day. That's an amazing insight and so useful for us to know.

My mother, an avid quilter, has a handstitched decoration over one of her sewing machines that reads, "A Day Hemmed in Prayer Seldom Unravels." Scripture, experience, and research establish the truth in this. We see accounts of King David (prolific writer of many Psalms, a man after God's own heart, and the first king appointed by God over His nation, Israel) as well as Jesus repeatedly committing morning hours to prayer.

Please hear me: I am not suggesting that the morning is when we should always schedule our prayer time or Bible study. I am suggesting, however, that every morning we should use those first few minutes of the day wisely and commit the day to the LORD with a brief prayer, scripture reading, meditation with the Holy Spirit, worship song, or similar focused moment of our choice—even if only for three minutes. Let's not allow the first few moments of our day to be hijacked by the current message, headline, or notification from our iPhone or television. We want anticipation for God, rather than the concerns of the world, to flood our hearts and minds each morning.

Let's be purposeful in how our day begins so that throughout the day we can better recognize that it is truly the day God has made, and we can be better positioned mentally and spiritually to rejoice and be glad in it.

MY VOICE, HIS HEART

What do the first few moments of each day usually include for you?

☐ Anxious thoughts ☐ Coffee ☐ Emails ☐ Shower

☐ Cooking breakfast ☐ Headlines ☐ Music ☐ Children

☐ Talking with spouse ☐ _____

What ideas do you have for reclaiming those first few moments of each day?

_____

_____

_____

_____

I want to encourage you that as you grow in relationship with our Heavenly Father, you'll find that mornings, and life overall, become brighter. I wore the Christian label across my forehead (figuratively speaking, of course) until I was into my late twenties. I was brought up in a Christian home and believed the teachings to be true, but I defined success according to the world's standards and lived accordingly. Christianity was a wholesome religion, not a winsome relationship. Church was a chore rather than a cherished delight. I understood God was a personal God in general, but I never imagined He was intimately aware and personally involved in every individual life.

However, when I began pressing into my relationship with God in prayer and study, I began waking up in the morning singing hymns and praise songs. This was a most stunning experience for me. When I found the scripture in Zephaniah 3:17, "He will rejoice over you with gladness...He will exult [delight] over you with loud singing," I supposed that God was singing over me as I slept and, as my spirit harmonized with His, I would awake with a song on my lips. I looked forward to my mornings, excited to discover what song I would be singing when I awoke.

You will have similar experiences. I don't know what they will be. But I can promise, they'll be especially fitting to delight and surprise *you*.

WEEK 1: INTRODUCTION TO PRAYER, DAY 4

Have you already had something similar happen that you would be willing to share?

_____

_____

_____

_____

A PERSONAL LOOK

If you were to grab my Bible and look through its pages, you might notice that Psalm 91 is one of the most marked up and highlighted scripture passages. God has directed me back to this Psalm at several times in my life. One of my dearest friends would tell you that in her Bible, Psalm 16 has almost no words that haven't been underlined, highlighted, or commented next to.

We have only one day left in this week together and I cannot bear to go further without asking you to open your Bible with me. Please turn to either Psalm 16, Psalm 91, or your personal favorite, and underline a single scripture that you will pray back to God in our closing prayer today. I will do the same. Take a moment and write those few words of scripture below to be included in our closing prayer together.

Taken from Psalm _____: "_____

_____

_____

_____

_____."

MY VOICE, HIS HEART

CLOSING PRAYER

"Most High God, Heavenly Father, Lord of my life, draw me into Your love and grow me in relationship with You. Tether my heart to Yours and show me the wonder of Your great love. Be quick to help me when I stumble, show me Your extended hand when I fall, begin in me a new work that would reclaim each day one by one. Strengthen my spirit with Your Spirit, from morning to morning.
[*Private words from your selected Psalm here.*]
I praise You and thank You for Your love over me, Your life in me, and especially for the sacrifice of Your Son, Jesus. Amen."[11]

DAY 5

Week 1: Introduction to Prayer

"Father in Heaven, You are the source of life, love and truth. Forgive me for being distracted, deceived, and blinded by this world to the reality of Who You are and who I am in You. Forgive me for forfeiting the joy and delight You offer to pursue worthless pleasures. Reform my life, refashion my heart, and transform my mind with Your truth and unfailing love. My hope is in You alone. In Jesus' name, amen."[12]

AN INTIMATE CONVERSATION

Here we are at the end of week one—well done! God's heart is bursting for you. Thank you for your perseverance in this pursuit. Your loving commitment is a bright light God will use to draw others to Himself.

Are you getting more comfortable with prayer? On a scale of 1 to 10, with 1 being "I am super uncomfortable and moving forward through a sheer act of will," and 10 being "I am loving this and can't wait for week two!" please draw a happy face to indicate where you are.

1..10

I long to see how you're feeling about your progress. I hope you're closer to 10, but I applaud your perseverance and happy face even if you are struggling and close to 1. Hebrews 11:6 tells us that God rewards those who diligently seek Him. So whether you are struggling or soaring like an eagle through this study, you have a reward, my beautiful friend—a reward that cannot tarnish or be taken away.

Intimate conversations are honest conversations. They lack the pretense and restraint of most casual conversations. One of the greatest joys of our relationship with God is that every prayer is an intimate conversation. We cannot pretend with God. He knows us better than we know ourselves. This sets us free to share deeply, honestly, and openly with Him.

MY VOICE, HIS HEART

One of the beautiful mysteries of prayer is that as we are intimate with God, He will not only reveal Himself to us more fully, but He will reveal our true selves to us more fully. As we come to see ourselves rightly, who we are through Him, we begin to transform more and more into the likeness of who He created us to be.

I look back at who I was before I began pursuing a relationship with God in prayer, and I hardly recognize myself. I am desperately aware of how I conducted my life back then, what I believed and valued—and my blind hypocrisy astounds me still. But I don't waste time on shame; instead, I focus only on gratefulness that God pursued me first and refused to leave me where I was. I didn't know I needed changing, and certainly transformation was not what I had in mind; but God knew, and through these intimate moments He has had His way in my heart, my will, and my life.

He longs to do the same with you. Intimate conversations are honest conversations. They will gently transform you from the inside out.

Are there some intimate, honest conversations you know you need to have with God?

☐ Yes ☐ No ☐ I'm not sure

Are you willing to have the intimate, honest conversations God leads you to share with Him, even if you aren't sure what they might be right now?

☐ Yes ☐ No ☐ I'm not sure

What are the most pressing topics or areas of your life that God is placing on your heart to share with Him during your conversations with Him?

_____

_____

_____

_____

WEEK 1: INTRODUCTION TO PRAYER, DAY 5

MY WILL VERSUS THY WILL

The book of Genesis gives us a glimpse into the intimate connection Adam enjoyed with God: daily walks together in the cool, open beauty of the garden; speaking face-to-face as God taught Adam how to care for and tend to what had been entrusted to him; working together with the plants and creatures; enjoying a relationship free from brokenness and shame.

Early on, God made it clear to Adam that He had gifted him with a uniquely independent will, unlike anything else in creation. God created Adam with the ability to not only understand God's will for him, but to choose whether to live in God's will or apart from it.

While in complete relationship together, Adam's will and God's will were in unity, aligned in harmony as one. When Adam chose to break apart and turn away from God's will for him and pursue a will opposed to God's will, the brokenness impacted all of creation. Adam's will, man's will, ceased to be one with God's will. God's will remained good, pure, and holy. Man's will became corrupted, unable to discern clearly or desire rightly.

In another garden, millennia later, we would see another wrestle with the will of man and the will of God. Jesus, in the Garden of Gethsemane—before he was betrayed by Judas, abandoned by his friends, beaten by soldiers, and nailed onto a cross—struggled in prayer. Jesus came into the world to heal the brokenness Adam had brought. Adam brought sin and death; Jesus bought redemption, forgiveness, and life.

In Genesis 3:6, we don't witness much struggle when Adam chose his will over God's will. With Jesus, we witness anguish and distress to the point of sweating blood as he faced the will of God, knowing he must choose for himself. Jesus pleads with God to make another way, to remove the path before him; yet he closes his prayer with these life-changing words: "not my will, but yours, be done."[13]

Adam chose "my will;" Jesus chose "Thy will." In prayer, we face the same struggle. Will we pursue "my will," asking God to _conform to us_, or will we pursue "Thy will," asking God to _conform us_?

MY VOICE, HIS HEART

We cannot be surprised when prayer is difficult. The more our will is out of line with God's will, or the more difficult the work God is asking us to step into, the more challenging prayer may become.

Take heart. Jesus has cleared the path for us and made a way for our will to once again be in unity with God's will. Through Christ we can enjoy the oneness of that intimate connection.

Do you believe this is possible? Do you believe your will can be in unity with God's will?

☐ Yes, absolutely   ☐ No, I don't think so   ☐ Hmm...still thinking

If you aren't quite there yet, I can't wait to show you something in scripture. If you are already right there with me, this is going to put a big smile on your face. Grab your Bible and flip over to John 17:20-26 and have a read. You may want to highlight this. I'll wait.

How many times does Christ request that we be brought to a "oneness," or to unity, with Him and the Father?

☐ 1 time   ☐ 2 times   ☐ 3 times   ☐ 4 times   ☐ 5 times

Do you see? Before He went to the cross to pay the penalty for my sin and yours, Christ Himself prayed for you to be one with Him and one with the Father—perfect unity. He prays not only once but three times, if I count right—and possibly more if we're not too picky about wording. I love the beauty and passion of the NIV translation in conveying Jesus' closing words as He foretells the coming of the Holy Spirit, saying, "that I myself may be in them."[14] You, my amazing friend, are made for One like no other one. Prayer works! Let's not shy away from a little hard work. The benefits are out of this world!

AN INTIMATE CONVERSATION IN SCRIPTURE

We can get hung up on trying to find the right words when talking with someone. Writing to someone can be even more of a challenge. My husband will often make fun of me because I spend an hour composing an email that he would spend five minutes on at most. I want each word to be clear, to connect, to convey what I intend.

WEEK 1: INTRODUCTION TO PRAYER, DAY 5

Written word lacks the vocal tone and facial and physical expressions that assist in translating the intent and spirit of a given communication. Research shows that people are more likely to read negative intent rather than positive intent into written communications, such as social media posts, texts, and emails. We have to be overly positive in our word selection to simply have the communication register as "not negative."

When we go to God's Word in scripture, we can know with full assurance that every word on every page is steeped in love, truth, grace, goodness, kindness, joy, and peace for all who will receive it. If we are ever at a loss for words and struggling to find the right ones in prayer, we can never go wrong with turning to scripture and praying the words God Himself has already gifted to us.

If you find yourself overwhelmed with a sense of feeling burdened, insufficient, unloved, fearful, ashamed...head straight to God's Word. Find a Psalm and give voice to the words, speaking each one personally, not as the prayer of another but as your personal words to your loving Father, and as His personal promise to you. Psalm 139 is my favorite Psalm to pray from beginning to end. The words pierce my heart afresh each time and my spirit rises with the truth of each word.

We will close this week uniting our words with God's Word, bringing our will into His perfect will for us. Turn to Psalm 139 in your Bible, and give your voice to scripture, knowing it is transforming your heart as it rises to His throne like beautiful incense brought to Him from the daughter He adores.

"Oh LORD, You have searched me..."
Give voice to Psalm 139.

Day and night they never stop saying: "Holy, holy, holy is the LORD God Almighty," who was, and is, and is to come.
REVELATION 4:8B

Our purpose is to love God completely, to love self correctly, and to love others compassionately.
KENNETH D. BOA

Week Two

DAY 1

Week 2: Adoration

OPENING PRAYER

"Gracious Father, my Redeemer, Shepherd and King—LORD, You are the Everlasting God, the Creator of all the earth. You created the heavens and the earth, the sea, and everything in them. You created everything that exists and through You everything has its being. You are the Alpha and Omega, the beginning and the end. You never grow weak or weary. No one can measure the depths of Your understanding. You give wisdom to all who ask. You are my banner and shield, my strength and protection. To You be all glory forever and ever. Amen."[1]

INFINITE, ALL POWERFUL, EVER PRESENT…GOD

Before we go further, we need to make sure we have the right perspective on a key principle: infinity. Buzz Lightyear, the much-loved character in the *Toy Story* movies, famously says, "To infinity…and beyond!" This was the most famous catchphrase in movie history, according to a 2014 poll.

The idea of infinity strikes a chord within us. It's not just child's play; it's as real as the breath we breathe, and understanding it rightly can change our prayer life significantly. We cannot see infinity, and it's hard for us to imagine, yet it's as simple as salt to God.

Infinity is the door to impossible possibilities when we have the right perspective. Let's see if we can adjust our perspective on infinity.

MY VOICE, HIS HEART

Grab a pen and draw a line below with two fixed end points. I'll wait.

Now <u>below</u> that line, indicate three different spans of time the line could represent. Specify a short time span, a longer time span, and an incredibly long time span. For example, my line could represent 15 minutes (the length of today's study time), 10 years (the length of time I have spent on radio), or 400 years (the anniversary of the Mayflower Compact).

<u>Above</u> this first line, draw a second line with <u>two fixed end points</u> that extends beyond the first line, almost to the edges of the page.

<u>Finally, above the second line</u> draw a third and final line that <u>extends off both edges of the page</u>—a line that has no fixed beginning or ending points.

You and I and all of humanity exist on the first timeline. Every span of time that you and I might consider significant, our daily lives, snapshot 15-minute experiences, and the entirety of man's history, takes place on this line. We can see by experience, historical record, or other scientific evidence that this timeline has some starting and ending point. We can look up and get a glimpse and recognize that the other two timelines exist, but because their beginning and end points extend beyond our own, we cannot see where they begin or where they end. From our vantage point on the first timeline, both timelines appear to be infinite, even though the second timeline is not. It, too, has a fixed beginning and end.

The enemy of our souls exists on the second timeline. Satan is not infinite like God. He is a created, finite being and he has a definite and promised end. Not only will Satan come to an end, but sin and the curse of death (the result of Satan's entire body of work) will come to a final, inescapable end. Amen!

God exists on the third timeline that runs off both ends of the page. Our Almighty God has no beginning and no end. He is an infinite, eternal Being.

WEEK 2: ADORATION, DAY 1

His power is infinite. His knowledge is infinite. His presence is infinite. There is no place or time that exists that He is not.

However, there are many New Age philosophies and religions which will want to convince us that good and evil are equal, opposing forces. This is a big lie; but please hear me, it is an understandable lie accepted by those who do not know God and who do not understand Him as infinite and eternal Creator of all things seen and unseen. If you encounter the yin-yang symbol or hear a teaching that Satan and Jesus are actually brothers, remember: man looks at both timelines which extend beyond his own existence, and they both appear to be infinite even though only one of them is. Praise God that we now know better.

A more perfect illustration for all this might be to draw the two fixed-point timelines and then establish God, not as a single infinite line but as every possible set of infinite lines both on the page and off, in every possible dimension and space: on, in, surrounding, above, below, through, throughout, and present. God is far greater than we can ever hope to imagine.

I don't know how to draw that, though. I hope this more simple analogy will still work to help us get the right perspective on how great is our God. More than we can ever know, He is greater than any foe, any fear, or any thing you and I will ever come up against.

Understanding this truth is vital. Satan, his existence, his power, his work, his influence, his hold—everything about him—is finite, fixed, limited, partial, reduced, restricted, and every other synonym you can put in here. Help me out. Any other synonyms come to mind?

_____

_____

_____

Are you getting this with me? Sin, and the enemy who brought it, are *less than* in every way. God and His goodness are *greater than* in every way, in more ways than you or I can imagine.

MY VOICE, HIS HEART

When I realized this, it was a game changer for me. I don't have to wring my hands and fret over the ways of the world, the hardship, the impending disaster, or what power Satan may wield. The enemy and sin have no power over me as a daughter of the One True God, and are nothing of consequence compared to the all-surpassing greatness of God. When I stand in my own power, I stand in a small, finite strength of will and am easily knocked down and around by the enemy; but when I stand in the power of Christ, I stand in the infinite, eternal, all-powerful, all-things-are-possible will of God. Today, He calls us into a deeper relationship with Him.

What Brings You Here?

There are no wrong reasons for turning to God in prayer. Anything that brings us to seek God has value. Why are you here?

☐ Scripture	☐ Desperation	☐ Friend	☐ Needs	☐ Hurt
☐ Curiosity	☐ Interest	☐ Job	☐ Children	☐ Desire
☐ To learn	☐ Anxiety	☐ Pain	☐ Fear	☐ Spouse
☐ Leadership	☐ Relationship	☐ Other _____		

What Has Kept You Away?

I am grateful for what you have overcome to get here today. I'm not sure ticking a box will do ample justice to share what has happened in your life to keep you from approaching God and engaging in an intimate relationship with Him, but it's all we can do right now. Sometimes God uses the same things that have kept us from Him to finally draw us to Him. Would you please share what has kept you away? You can then be aware that these things might keep you away in the future. You can prayerfully address them with God, and hold yourself accountable to make sure they do not keep you from His loving presence again.

☐ Time	☐ Addiction	☐ Education	☐ Needs	☐ Hurt
☐ Priorities	☐ Family	☐ Shame	☐ Background	☐ Fear
☐ Experience	☐ Schedule	☐ Spouse	☐ Pain	☐ Career
☐ Disinterest	☐ Job	☐ Other _____		

WEEK 2: ADORATION, DAY 1

What brings us to seek God in prayer may change from week to week depending on our circumstances and life surprises. However, there seems to be one deterrent that likely few of us marked but almost all of us experience in the background of our thoughts. We may not have been able to accurately identify it until now, but we need to acknowledge it: shame.

I find that shame pushes me away from spending time with God in prayer rather than driving me towards Him. Yet shame hides in the shadows, often difficult to identify. We should experience healthy conviction—that which arises from an attentive spirit and acknowledges the guilt of sin in our life and drives us towards God in repentance and healthy change. A spirit of shame is based on a false standard of prideful perfectionism which becomes a destructive way of thinking, never leading to healthy change but instead to the false belief of worthlessness, hopelessness, and failure.

Shame says, "You aren't good enough to do this;" "You made a commitment that you'll never keep;" "You're such a fake;" or, "How many times are you going to try this before you give up like you always do?" I could fill pages with all the lies shame has whispered to discourage me. What about you? What lies does shame whisper in the back of your thoughts?

_____

_____

_____

_____

We will no longer allow shame to keep us from God. Psalm 22:5 promises that when God's children trust in Him, they will not be put to shame. Our minds and our lives are not to be filled with shame. Let us reject the discouraging whispers of shame and embrace the encouraging whispers of God. We may be put to use, put to rest, or put to the test. But as we trust in God, we will never be put to shame.

APPROACHING GOD, KNOWING HIS RESPONSE

When an acquaintance shows up unexpectedly on our doorstep, we can't

MY VOICE, HIS HEART

help but wonder what brings her. Our mind may run through a vast array of scenarios to anticipate what is going on: Have I forgotten a commitment? Are they okay? Do they need something?

On the other hand, if it's a dear friend who shows up unexpectedly on our doorstep, delight will likely be our first response as we throw open the door and rush out to hug her. This is a wonderful visit no matter what circumstances prompted her to come.

I want to tell you that God's response when we pray is always the latter response. He knows we are living in a hurtful, challenging world that tends to bang up the best of His warriors. There is nothing that has escaped His notice—especially not you, not even for a second.

As we close in prayer today, open the eyes of your heart to see God gladly receiving you as you approach Him in prayer. Let's refer back to what we have acknowledged above and be open with Him about what <u>brings us</u> and what has <u>kept us away</u>.

CLOSING PRAYER

"Gracious God, in Your everlasting arms I rest securely, shielded and protected. You have called me out of this world and into an intimate relationship with You. That is too wonderful for me to comprehend.
[Acknowledge in your own words what has brought you to Him today.]
I am overwhelmed by Your love for me. Thank You for drawing me to You. For too long, I have pursued my own will and lived apart from You.
[Acknowledge in your own words what has kept you away.]
Forgive me for my selfish ways. I turn to You fully. I desire the oneness in relationship with You that Jesus requested on my behalf. Teach me to walk in Your ways, to abide in Your will, and to rest in Your unfailing love. In Jesus' name, amen."[2]

WEEK 2: ADORATION, DAY

DAY 2

Week 2: Adoration

OPENING PRAYER

"LORD God, my Rock, You are perfect in all Your ways. You are just and righteous. You are a God of faithfulness, without wrong-doing. In You is all wisdom and understanding. You have formed man from the dust of the earth. You have appointed times for the nations. Nothing can stand against You. You have claimed me as Your own. You uphold me with Your righteous right hand and give me strength to stand. Forgive my sins, for I have sinned against You alone. Thank You for Your mercy and gentleness. In Jesus' name, amen."[3]

PRAYER PERFECTION

God has not given the gift of prayer to only a few but to ALL. We learned this truth last week but it is worth repeating. If prayer is for everyone, why would a Bible study on prayer ever be needed? Great question, and one I have asked myself.

One of my closest friend's husband is a sleep doctor. When she first told me his profession, I thought she was joking with me. How could anyone make a living as a sleep doctor? Why would anyone need to invest ten years to be educated on sleep? Everyone sleeps; our bodies are made to require sleep. It's not difficult: put on comfy pajamas, fluff your pillow, turn out the lights, lay down your head, and voilà—sweet dreams. I could be a sleep doctor!

And yet...I've come to realize that there is much more to it than that. While our bodies are created in such a way as to need sleep in order to be physically healthy, few people actually sleep well at night.

Likewise, prayer is needed for spiritual health. Our spirits are designed to be in relationship with our Creator. Often, we attempt to fill that need with substitutes. However, our need for God cannot be met by anyone or anything but God Himself. Thankfully, we don't require ten years of education to be able to pray effectively, or to help others do the same.

MY VOICE, HIS HEART

While teaching someone to pray may seem equally ludicrous as teaching someone how to sleep, it is also the surest way to impact positive change in someone's life. As sleep can help restore one's physical strength and health, so too does prayer have the same result spiritually.

Did you need someone to teach you how to talk to your mom, your dad, your siblings? No, of course not; you simply spoke to them because they were with you and you had a desire to communicate. Then why would anyone need to teach us how to talk to God?

I believe sometimes we simply lack the belief that He is truly with us. God made sure to give us a specific assurance that He is with us by establishing this very name for His Son upon birth: "Behold, the virgin shall conceive and bear a son, and they shall call his name Immanuel (which means, God with us)."[4] Possibly this is the first truth regarding prayer that we need to work deep into our spirits: God is with us.

The greatest teacher on prayer was Jesus. He modeled a life of prayer and taught more on having a healthy relationship with the Father than anything else in His three years of ministry. As Jews, the disciples had been brought up praying at least three times every day since they were toddlers; yet, they specifically asked Jesus to teach them to pray. I am forever grateful God made sure to have Matthew and Luke include the historical account of this.

Open up with me to Matthew 6:9 or Luke 11:1 in your Bible and read the prayer Jesus models for His disciples.

How long was this model prayer Jesus provided?

☐ 4 pages ☐ 4 paragraphs ☐ 4 sentences

Would you say the prayer Jesus provided was simple and easy to understand or complex and beyond the disciples' grasp?

___

WEEK 2: ADORATION, DAY 2

Is this the only prayer Jesus prayed in front of His disciples?

- ☐ I think so.
- ☐ No, He prayed one or two other times in front of them.
- ☐ No, Jesus prayed several times in public, both in the synagogue and in front of His disciples.

Is this the only time Jesus taught about prayer to His disciples and others?

- ☐ I think so.
- ☐ No, He taught one or two other times on prayer.
- ☐ Jesus taught on prayer several times in public, both in the synagogue and to His disciples.

I imagine the disciples around Jesus were excited to learn how to pray like Him. They were surely expecting a great sermon, teaching them how to claim victory, defeat the enemy, move mountains, and gain special access to the power of God. Yet what they got was a profoundly humble, 30-second, 4-sentence prayer. And here is the kicker: Jesus then turns the tables and begins teaching for the next hour (almost 50 verses) on matters of the heart—how to live, character issues, morality issues, spiritual belief, relationship with God and relationship with others. Oof, that must have been unexpected and, dare I say it, unwanted.

Like the disciples, we, too, need to understand that it's not the eloquence of the words or the length of the prayer, but the heart of the sinner that matters most. Impressive words do not gain us access to the throne of God and eloquence does not attune His ear; only a humble heart submitted to Him is received. So take heart! Stumbling, simple words are beautiful to God. This sets me free. How about you?

PICTURE PERFECT

What do you picture when you pray? What do you envision with your mind's eye as you bow your head or clasp your hands? Share with me any pictures or images that tend to come to mind for you when you pray. I have provided some visuals that are either personal to me or have been shared with me by other women over the years. Please checkmark any of the visuals that appeal to you personally or add your own.

MY VOICE, HIS HEART

- ☐ Jesus standing (or sitting) next to me.
- ☐ Bright light of heaven.
- ☐ God leaning down to listen to me.
- ☐ God sitting on His throne.
- ☐ The Father's holy face smiling, knowing me, full of wisdom, love, and grace.
- ☐ A green field, next to water, with mountains in the distance and me sitting down peacefully in it, surrounded by the loving presence of God.
- ☐ A mountain top with me sitting down next to Jesus, overlooking the vastness of the cities and valleys in the distance.
- ☐ Heaven, with gold streets, grape vines bursting with fruit, trees full of ripe fruit of every kind, a shimmery river running briskly by, and angels singing.
- ☐ People's faces as I pray for them.
- ☐ My family standing together in unity holding hands.
- ☐ My family members in heaven, standing with smiles and love near Jesus.
- ☐ The church all over the world standing together in prayer and me among them.
- ☐ Nothing. My mind is generally focused on praying and I don't picture anything.
- ☐ _____

When I ask women what they picture when they pray, I usually get one of three immediate responses: a huge smile; a thoughtful "I'm processing" kind of look; or a blank stare. Please know there is no right answer. If there were, surely Jesus would have told us what it should be.

Remember, we must know one truth throughout our being: We are not praying into a void but to a living Person. That Person is perfect in every possible way. He is perfection beyond any ideal we can ever imagine. He is with us and He. Loves. Us.

WEEK 2: ADORATION, DAY 2

When we pray, we don't need to understand God fully. In fact, that's impossible. But we do need to understand God rightly. He is not wandering about wringing His hands over the mess humans have made. He is Sovereign, firmly seated on the throne of heaven, understanding entirely all of creation. He is all powerful, and is bringing together everything happening in every inch of creation to work according to His plan for the ultimate good of His children.

He is perfect. His will is perfect. His love is perfect. Whatever we picture when we pray, we should picture *perfect* when we picture our Heavenly Father, God.

Here are just a few of the scriptures that declare the perfection of God. Would you complete each scripture by writing in the missing word in each? I'll save you some time if you are pressed for minutes today: Every missing word is "perfect." If you have the time, highlight these scriptures in your Bible.

Deuteronomy 32:4: "The Rock, His work is _____, for all His ways are justice. A God of faithfulness and without iniquity, just and upright is He."

Job 36:4: "For truly my words are not false; one who is _____ in knowledge is with you."

Psalm 18:30: "This God—His way is _____; the word of the LORD proves true; He is a shield for all those who take refuge in Him."

Psalm 19:7: "The law of the Lord is _____, reviving the soul; the testimony of the Lord is sure, making wise the simple."

Romans 12:2b: "Then you will be able to test and approve what God's will is; His good, pleasing and _____ will."

PERFECTLY LOVED

Let us also see ourselves rightly when we pray. We obviously are not perfect; however, we are perfectly accepted, valued, and loved by God. He has pulled us up out of the ditch (or whatever gutter or deep, dark well we may have been in) and He has cleaned us and placed a beautiful white robe over us. We are not beggars, but children—fully adopted with every right as an heir.[5]

Finally, let us see the world and our circumstances rightly through God's eyes. He knows that both are temporary and neither are random. The world and our circumstances do not determine or define who God is; it is He Who sets limits, determines outcomes, and directs the course of history. We cannot permit our experiences to define God; we must have God define our experiences.

His hand is present and active; we need only open our eyes to see and our heart to trust. We need not wonder, "How will I survive this?" We can, instead, take an eternal perspective—His perspective—and proclaim to Him, "Do mighty works with this according to Your perfect will, Father; and if You would have me survive it, strengthen me through it." Take hold of courage, knowing He is over all that concerns you. He is with you and for you.

INTERACTIVE PRAYER DOWNLOAD

If you are using the Let's Pray Today Ministries "Prayer for Beginners" mp3 download, go to Prayer #1 on Track 2. Listen and pray all the way through to the end of Prayer #1 (approx. 7 minutes). You may use that prayer as your closing prayer for today, or you can pray through today's closing prayer as well. Your choice, friend.

CLOSING PRAYER

"Heavenly Father, help me to see rightly through Your eyes. Correct my vision and give me eyes to see Your hand at work in my life and in everything around me. You are perfect. Your ways are perfect. In You I am made perfect, not of my doing but through Your Son Jesus, who is alive and at work in me.

Right now I am struggling with [*insert your own words here*].

Take these struggles. I give them to You. I place them in Your hands. Give me the rest and peace You have promised as I place my trust in You. In Jesus' name, amen."[6]

DAY 3

Week 2: Adoration

OPENING PRAYER

Would you please open us in prayer today? Write out your prayer below and then go back and pray it out loud.

"Gracious God, _____

_____

_____

_____

_____

_____. In Jesus' name I pray. Amen."

I would love to hear your prayer! If you want to share it, send it to me. If it's just between you and our Heavenly Father, enjoy your intimate time with Him.

PERFECT POSTURE

My youngest is a former gymnast and my middle child loves jumping horses. Both have excellent posture. I, however, do not. When I was in my 30s, I was stopped by a stranger in the locker room of my local gym, who told me I was going to end up a slumped over old lady if I didn't work on my posture. As I stood there half dressed, I had to laugh because my great-grandmother had spoken almost the same words to me on many occasions in my teenage years.

I thanked the woman and we talked for another 20 minutes. She walked me through some exercises (after I put my shirt on) and posture awareness triggers to help me work toward a more ideal standing position. Let's just say I've learned a lot about posture over the years.

MY VOICE, HIS HEART

During time in ministry and radio, women have come up and asked me, "How do I pray?" This question can hold an array of different meanings, so my first response is, "Help me to understand what you mean." At least a third of the time, ladies are inquiring about prayer posture. They want to know the perfect posture one ought to assume when praying to God.

Thankfully, prayer does not require perfect posture of any sort. There is no physical stance one must take in order to be heard or for one's prayers to be most effective. However, what we choose to do with our hands, head, eyes, and legs may be an indication of what is going on within us spiritually.

Let's see first what scripture says about physical stance or posture when praying. Then we'll talk about historical church practices and cultural traditions. Finally, you'll get to choose for yourself.

Look up each scripture in your Bible and fill in the missing words in the following verses. For these I used my NIV[7] Bible. If you want to check your answers, they are listed in the Appendix (p. 219). I encourage you to open your Bible and enjoy finding these small treasures.

HANDS

Psalm 28:2: "Hear my cry for _____ as I call to you for _____, as I lift up my _____ toward your Most Holy Place."

Psalm 134:2: "Lift up your _____ in the sanctuary and _____ the LORD."

Lamentations 2:19: "Arise, _____ _____ in the night, as the watches of the night begin; pour out your _____ like water in the presence of the Lord. Lift up your _____ to him for the lives of your children, who faint from hunger at every street corner."

1 Timothy 2:8: "Therefore I want the men everywhere to pray, lifting up _____ _____ without anger or disputing."

1 Kings 8:22-23a: "Then Solomon _____ before the altar of the

WEEK 2: ADORATION, DAY 3

LORD in front of the whole assembly of Israel, spread out his _____
_____ _____ and said…"

Psalm 141:2: "May my prayer be set before you like incense; may the _____ up of my _____ be like the evening sacrifice."

Matthew 19:13: "Then people brought little children to Jesus for him to place his _____ on them and _____ for them."

EYES

Psalm 123:1: "I _____ up my _____ to you, to you who sit enthroned in heaven."

John 17:1a: "After Jesus said this, he_____ _____ _____ and prayed…"

LEGS

Mark 11:25: "And whenever you _____ praying, if you have anything against anyone, forgive him, that your Father in heaven may also forgive you your trespasses.

1 Samuel 1:26: "And she said to him, "Pardon me, my lord. As surely as you live, I am the woman who _____ here beside you, praying to the LORD.

1 Chronicles 17:16: "Then King David went in and _____ before the LORD, and he said: "Who am I, LORD God, and what is my family, that you have brought me this far?"

1 Kings 8:54: "When Solomon had _____ all these prayers and supplications to the LORD, he _____ from before the altar of the LORD, where he had been _____ with his_____ _____ _____ toward _____."

MY VOICE, HIS HEART

Ephesians 3:14: "For this reason I _____ before the Father."

POSTURE IN TIMES OF GREAT DISTRESS OR DIFFICULTY

Ezra 9:5b-6: "I ... fell on my _____ with my _____ _____ out to the LORD my God and prayed: I am too ashamed and disgraced, my God, to _____ up my _____ to you, because our sins are higher than our heads and our guilt has reached to the heavens."

Matthew 26:39: "he [Jesus] _____ with his _____ to the _____ and prayed, "My Father, if it is possible, may this cup be taken from me. Yet not as I will, but as you will."

Based on the above scriptures, what did people generally do with their hands during prayer? Check all that apply.

- ☐ Hands were clasped or held together under the chin, touching the forehead, or in one's lap.
- ☐ Hands were spread apart and held towards heaven.
- ☐ Hands were placed on those being prayed for.

Based on the above scriptures, what did people generally do with their eyes during prayer? Check all that apply.

- ☐ Eyes were generally closed and head was bowed.
- ☐ Eyes were often open and looking toward heaven.
- ☐ Eyes were sometimes lowered or face was placed on the ground in times of great difficulty or disgrace.

Based on the above scriptures, what did people generally do with their legs during prayer? Check all that apply.

- ☐ Standing, sitting, and kneeling were all used in prayer.
- ☐ Standing or kneeling with hands lifted to heaven while praying was common practice.
- ☐ Prostrate on the ground in times of great difficulty or disgrace was not unusual.

WEEK 2: ADORATION, DAY 3

The first time I went through a Bible search similar to this, it felt as though someone had ripped off a band-aid. Some of the prayer stances we have all been raised with are not actually practiced in the Bible or by the early church. That is okay. The body position we use today comes from some wonderful church traditions.

Again, let's remember: It is one's heart in prayer that God regards. Tomorrow we'll look at one of my favorite parables in scripture to prove this point. For now, let's consider from where our common prayer posture derived.

If you're like me, you were taught that sitting during prayer is most common, kneeling is better (but reserved mostly for the devout and repentant or for more serious moments in prayer), and to stand only if the pastor has specifically requested the congregation stand for a particular prayer together. Yet most accounts of prayer in the Bible involve standing or kneeling. Aside from Job 2:13 and 1 Chronicles 17:16, I have not found accounts of people sitting in prayer, unless you count blessing meals. There is an account of King Hezekiah on his death bed praying to God in Isaiah 38:2, and of King David lying on his bed thinking of God at night in Psalm 63:6, but otherwise standing and kneeling are the Biblical standard.

The *Orans* prayer posture is one you may have seen but not thought much about. *Orans* is a Medieval Latin word which means "one who is praying or pleading." This posture, used by the early church (and seen in a lot of early Christian art), usually consists of standing with the hands extended sideways, palms up and the elbows close to one's sides. Some faith groups still use this body position in prayer.

Bowing one's head, with eyes firmly shut and hands clasped, is what most of us have been taught. This is a wonderful way to pray, but quite different from the common accounts of prayer we find in scripture of hands raised towards heaven and eyes open. We have gone from an upward looking, standing, arms open posture to something far more submissive and pensive. Why might this be?

This transition to clasped hands and closed eyes in prayer came to the Western Church in the 1200s, a period of significant monastic influence. Hands folded or clasped together is symbolic of submission. Just as a slave's hands would be bound or shackled together, we approach God as humble servants, submitting our will to His, acknowledging Him as Lord.

MY VOICE, HIS HEART

As for bowing one's head, we might understand this better by shifting our perspective. We can think of it as lowering one's eyes in humility. Lifting our face to heaven is fine and beautiful; lowering our eyes in humility is also good and right.

Our body language in prayer is a language God certainly understands. If you want to lift your hands to heaven and tell God how much you love Him, lift them high and smile as big as you can. If you are wrestling with submitting your plans to His will for your life, you might prefer a different posture in prayer. You decide; there is no right or wrong. This is something for which I personally will forever be grateful: in prayer we need never worry about perfect posture!

As we close in prayer today, enjoy your time with God. Maybe you want to try a new posture you have never tried before. It is also fine to stick with what you're most comfortable with. Your choice. After you pray, quiet your heart and mind and listen as He gently shares His heart with you and wraps you in His love.

CLOSING PRAYER

"Heavenly Father, You delight in Your children. As I draw near to You in prayer, You draw near to me in Your mercy and grace. Thank You for inviting me into relationship with You. Thank You for surrounding me in Your love.
Forgive my wandering heart, LORD. Take it and bind it to Yours. Clean me, Father, and I will be clean. Correct me and lead me on Your path of life and love all the days You have appointed for me. Pour out Your love into my heart and over my whole being. I love You and I delight in Your love for me. I pray in the precious name of Jesus. Amen."[8]
[*Quietly listen and be in the Father's presence.*]

WEEK 2: ADORATION, DAY

DAY 4

Week 2: Adoration

OPENING PRAYER

"How can I approach the throne of God? You, Father, are holy and I am not. Through Christ You have made a way. You, Lord Jesus, are my salvation. You are my light and my hope in this dark world. You are the stronghold of my life. You, LORD, prepare a place for me. Even in the presence of my enemies I am safe, for You are with me. You will never leave or abandon me. I approach the throne of my Father, God, Who welcomes me into His presence as a beloved daughter, a valued servant, a beautiful bride. I thank You for Your mercy that forgives, Your grace that gives, and Your love that never ends. In Jesus' name, amen."[9]

THE HEART OF THE MATTER

One of my favorite books in the Bible (as you may have already guessed) is Psalms. Of the 150 that exist, King David single-handedly composed roughly half. The Psalms, though poetic, are beautifully relatable and easy to understand. David speaks straight from his heart, full of emotion and metaphor, yet tells it like it is. He holds nothing back regarding his circumstances, difficulties, or struggles. He acknowledges and reflects on the truth of who God is; and in doing so, turns his moaning to praise and his struggles to joy. He relates to God. He appeals to God. He turns to God to both praise Him and seek refuge.

While David's words may seem eloquent to us, it is the simple expression of his heart which is truly remarkable. When God chose David to be king over Israel, no one could believe it, not even the prophet Samuel who served God night and day in the tabernacle. God spoke to Samuel and pointed out that while man looks on the outward appearance, God looks on the heart. We do not ever need to be concerned with composing the right words in prayer. God does not need poetic flattery or a well-prepared metaphor. He looks on the heart. Are you willing to share yours openly with Him?

☐ Yes I am   ☐ I am working on it.

MY VOICE, HIS HEART

I want to further prove this point. Jesus shared a parable to directly address the importance of one's heart in prayer. Jesus compares the prayers of two men and how they are received by God. Let's see what God will teach us. Please fill in the key words:

Luke 18:9-14 (NIV):

"To some who were confident of their own _____ and looked down on everyone else, Jesus told this parable: "Two men went up to the temple to pray, one a _____ and the other a _____ _____. The Pharisee stood by himself and prayed: 'God, I thank you that I am not like other _____—robbers, evildoers, and adulterers—or even like this tax collector. I fast twice a week and give a tenth of all I get.'

"But the _____ _____ stood at a distance. He would not even _____ _____ to heaven, but beat his breast and said, 'God, have mercy on me, a _____.'

"I tell you that this man, rather than the other, went home _____ before God. For all those who _____ themselves will be humbled and those who _____ themselves will be exalted."

1. Where are both men praying?
- ☐ In their homes
- ☐ At the temple
- ☐ In a garden

2. Are the men speaking their prayers or praying silently?
- ☐ Both are speaking
- ☐ Both are silent prayers
- ☐ One is audible and the other is silent

3. Are they standing, kneeling, sitting or prostrate?
- ☐ Both are standing
- ☐ Both are kneeling
- ☐ One is standing and the other is sitting

WEEK 2: ADORATION, DAY 4

4. Are they looking heavenward or turning their faces down?

☐ Both are looking up to heaven
☐ Both are facing down
☐ One is face up and the other is face down

5. How many words did the Pharisee pray?

☐ Quite a few
☐ Almost five times more than the tax collector
☐ 33
☐ All of these

6. How many words did the tax collector pray?

☐ Very few
☐ Seven
☐ Many less than the Pharisee
☐ All of these

These men are in the temple. This would be similar to you and I going to pray in our local church.

Both are standing, but did you notice that Jesus calls out the Pharisee for standing by himself? Pharisees were educated in the law of Moses and seen, in general, as spiritual leaders of the people. Some Pharisees were ministers, teachers, and priests from the high priestly line of Aaron. Yet instead of ministering in the temple, this Pharisee distances himself from someone he considers unworthy, even though that person has come to pray and is clearly repentant. Notice the tax collector is standing back, won't look up, and is beating his breast. This is pretty obvious body language.

Can you imagine walking into a church with the weight of the world heavy on your shoulders and the pastor of the church purposefully standing at a distance from you, without compassion and full of contempt? Would that experience bring you closer to God or discourage you? If you've had an experience like this, my heart breaks for you and I pray God will heal that wound. The overwhelming majority of pastors have hearts full of compassion. If you've had a bad experience in the church, would you share it on the next page and ask God to help you fully forgive the offense against you?

MY VOICE, HIS HEART

_____

_____

_____

_____

Now imagine walking into a church, burdened with loss, shame, or hardship, and as you stand near the altar to pray, a compassionate pastor approaches you and asks if he can pray with or for you. That experience is sure to bring you closer to God and encourage your socks off. I pray you have had that experience before. I have—and what a profound difference it made in this girl's life. If you have had a similar experience would you please share it?

_____

_____

_____

_____

I want to share an encouragement with you. Do you realize that once you get comfortable voicing prayers to God, you will be able to approach a person who is down and desperate for God? And you, my amazing friend, will be able to pray with her and be the light in her darkness, shining the love and compassion of Christ over her life! Wow. What a motivation for us to press into this relationship and grow in prayer.

The prayers of both the Pharisee and the tax collector are spoken. Jesus says so. Not surprising, as it was common practice in those times. Jesus also tells us they are both standing. The Pharisee prays reflecting on his good deeds and law-abiding status, and uses almost five times more words than the tax collector. The tax collector literally uses only seven words to unload what is on his heart at that moment. I imagine tears flowing from a broken man who is unable to speak another word to a God he knows is holy, righteous, and just.

WEEK 2: ADORATION, DAY 4

Let us shift our sight to our eternal eyes for a moment. The Pharisee believes he is righteous, standing near to God and at a good distance from sin (that is, the tax collector). On the other hand, the tax collector recognizes his sin and stands at a distance from the altar of God. Jesus teaches us that it is the Pharisee, who has lifted himself up in his own eyes, who is spiritually far from God. Consequently, the Pharisee departs the temple unforgiven, while the tax collector, who has recognized and confessed his sin, is spiritually near to God and departs forgiven.

Where are we fixing the eyes of our heart in prayer? Are we fixing our eyes on God or on man? Are we seeing ourselves (the good and the bad) as God sees us, or are we seeing ourselves (by comparison and judgement) through the eyes of man? Let's fix the eyes of our hearts on our holy God.

A SIMPLE EXPRESSION: A KISS FOR GOD

I have hesitated to employ this overused acronym but possibly it is well-used here. We have clearly seen that eloquence is unnecessary when we pray. While we are finding our words and finding our voice in prayer, let's Keep It Short and Simple. I would say keep it Short and Sweet but anytime we pray, it is already a sweet aroma to God. So let's go with Simple—straightforward and to the point, not beating around the bush or trying to impress God or others with flowery adjectives and sophisticated phrasing. I for one look forward to the day I can plant a big kiss on His beautiful, holy face. For now a KISS in prayer will be our delight—and His.

Jesus gave one direction about our words in prayer: While we are to be persistent in asking and not give up in prayer, we are not to engage in meaningless repetitions.[10] While repeating certain phrasings over and over again might convince our minds toward a given direction, we cannot convince God with words that repeatedly flow from our lips but never pass through the doorway of our heart. Prayers that are repeated merely to tick a box might end up ticking off more than we bargained for. As my dad might say, "More words do not better prayers make."

As we close in prayer, please refer back to the experience(s) you shared about praying in church. If you had a bad experience, it's time to share that with God and let Him set you free from the pain and allow forgiveness to flow into your heart for that pastor or servant who let you down. If you had a good experience, please share that with God and thank Him for the person who ministered to you and ask for a blessing over that individual.

Breathe in, big breath out, relax your shoulders. Enjoy your time with our wonderful God.

CLOSING PRAYER

"Father in Heaven, You have set Your eyes on me and delight in me as Your precious child. You fix Your eyes on my heart and You gently tend to what needs fixing. My innermost thoughts are not hidden from You. You do not reject me or abandon me. Your faithfulness is never ending.
Open my eyes to the works of Your hands, that Your goodness and beauty would be ever before me. You know of my hurts and my joys, and I want to share these with You now.
[*Share personal experiences.*]
Thank You, LORD, my God. In Jesus' holy name I pray, amen."[11]

DAY 5

Week 2: Adoration

OPENING PRAYER

"LORD, You have said that I will have difficulty in this world but that I am not to worry because You have overcome the world. You have said that You love me, provide for me, and give me good gifts. You have said that You do not give as the world gives, but You give freely and fully. You have said that in response to my prayers of thanksgiving and petition, Your peace will cover my heart and mind in Christ Jesus.
I trust You, Father, and I trust Your Word as truth. Teach me to build my life on Your strong foundation, as I place my life in Your mighty hands. This I ask in the powerful name of Jesus, the name above every other name in heaven and on earth. Amen."[12]

A HOLY HUG

Here we are at the end of Week 2. You are fabulous! I hope you are learning and growing in prayer through this study as much as I am. I want to hug you. I would even settle for leaning over to draw a heart on the back of your hand. Maybe you can do it for me on your own hand—or if you're in a group, draw a heart on the back of someone else's hand for me. I am going to stop and draw a heart on my hand from you. Now anytime someone asks you (or me) why on earth you have a heart on the back of your hand, that is our cue to give that person a big, holy hug from both of us. I will do the same; we'll be sisters in Christ, sharing the love of Christ with those around us. It is a good day to have a good day!

Speaking of holy hugs, in Day 5 last week, we looked at John 17, an incredible passage in scripture in which Christ references the coming of the Holy Spirit. Here Jesus is praying His final seven words of prayer with His disciples before He heads to the Garden of Gethsemane and prepares to offer His life to redeem ours. In this prayer Christ appeals to the Father, asking for unity and oneness among Himself, His followers, and the Father. Jesus' request is this: "that I myself may be in them."

MY VOICE, HIS HEART

This prayer was answered at Pentecost when the Holy Spirit came down to dwell personally in followers of Christ.[13] You and I are living in the answer to this prayer. That gives me chills. We, friend, are living as recipients of the Father's "Yes" to His Son's request. I have a "Yes!" living in me; He is the Holy Spirit of God.

Scripture tells us that He is the same Spirit of Christ.[14] If I could assign you any reading in the Bible it would be Romans 8. (I won't...but maybe you'll choose to go there on your own for an amazing ride. Prepare to have your mind blown and your spirit lit on fire if you do.) I will, however, have you highlight two very special verses in that chapter.

Romans 8:26-27 (NIV)
> "In the same way, the Spirit helps us in our weakness. We do not know what we ought to pray for, but the Spirit himself intercedes for us through wordless groans. And he who searches our hearts knows the mind of the Spirit, because the Spirit intercedes for God's people in accordance with the will of God.."

- Circle or highlight everywhere you see the word "Spirit."
- Square or highlight in another color everywhere you see the word "He."
- Triangle or highlight in a different color the word "God."

The Apostle Paul (who wrote the book of Romans) goes even further in verse 34 and encourages us all the more. He writes that while the Holy Spirit intercedes for our spirit, Christ Himself is at the right hand of God interceding for us before His Father.

Are you getting this? It may be obvious to you, but I went years not understanding this remarkable truth about prayer. In prayer the fullness of the Godhead—Spirit, Son (He), and Father (God)—is embracing us in a Holy Hug. I don't know any other activity for which scripture specifically calls out the full presence and engagement of God with man in this intimately personal and focused way. If you ever doubted that prayer is powerful and effective, you need not doubt any longer.

Did you happen to notice a key principle, which we have already learned, tucked away beautifully in last six words of Romans 8:27? I hope it caught your eye, if even for a brief moment. Go back and underline "according to the will of God." The Spirit and the Son both work "according to the will of God."

WEEK 2: ADORATION, DAY 5

Not my will, but Thy will, be done… This is a prayer that may come from our mouth, but the Spirit and Son would be in full agreement. When we align our will with God's will and we pray accordingly, our prayers are bound in powerful accord. Amazing. We are going to continue to learn more on this.

Another quick note for my friends who may use a different Bible translation or who like to engage in more in-depth study. Some translations use the word "Spirit" again rather than the word "He" in these two verses. However, the original Greek word used here for "He who searches" is only seen one other time in scripture, in Revelation chapter 2, where it is specifically used in reference to the Son of God. For this reason, I prefer the NIV translation, which more accurately uses "He" for this particular passage, refering to Christ, the Son of God. In the end, God is One, and that is an easy truth we can rely on when we have a hard time wrapping our finite minds around the more challenging truth that He is also three distinct Persons in perfect unity, love, and relationship.

A IS FOR ADORATION

Our prayers, our conversations with God, should not be forced. If we are told to adore God, yet we do not have a true sense of adoration for Him, the words simply are not going to be from our hearts. So what good would they be? For we know God is not interested in many words but in the integrity of our hearts.[15]

We've spent a week considering some pretty amazing qualities of God and the relationship He desires to have with us. Has anything caused you to pause or lose your breath for a moment? Is there anything that put a smile on your face or created a "Wow!" in your spirit? That is where you can begin adoring God in prayer.

My single favorite thing about God, aside from His personal love for me, is that God has made Himself <u>knowable</u> to us. This amazes me every time I ponder it. Our finite, created minds are able to grasp Who He is enough to have a meaningful, loving relationship with Him. He has also made Himself <u>known</u> to us. He didn't stop with simply creating us with the capacity to know Him, but He then purposefully reveals Himself to us. He does not hide Himself but has revealed His existence so plainly that those who refuse to acknowledge Him, He says, "are without excuse."[16] Let's keep our eyes open and fall more in love each day.

MY VOICE, HIS HEART

What are your favorite things about God? What WOWs you about HIm? Write down your top seven favorite qualities or characteristics.

1. _____

2. _____

3. _____

4. _____

5. _____

6. _____

7. _____

In 1992, Kay Arthur, one of my favorite Bible teachers, wrote a book exploring the names of God. The book won the Gold Book Award from the Evangelical Christian Publishers Association in 2019. Scripture records names that have been given to God by those who encountered Him personally and who stood in wonder, adoration, and awe. These names highlight God's character, qualities, and heart. Some of these names may resonate with you. Based on your experiences and relationship with Him, would you say any of these names are especially fitting or are names that you would personally give Him? Check any that stand out for you.

- ☐ God (*Elohim*)
- ☐ Lord God Almighty (*El Shaddai*)
- ☐ The Most High God (*El Elyon*)
- ☐ The Everlasting God (*El Olam*)
- ☐ The God Who Sees (*El Roi*)
- ☐ The LORD Who Heals (*Jehovah Rapha*)
- ☐ The LORD Who Sanctifies (*Jehovah Mekoddishkem*)
- ☐ The LORD Will Provide (*Jehovah Jireh*)
- ☐ The LORD Is Peace (*Jehovah Shalom*)
- ☐ The LORD of Hosts (*Jehovah Saboath*)
- ☐ God with Us (*Emmanuel*)
- ☐ LORD, Master (*Adonai*)

WEEK 2: ADORATION, DAY 5

- ☐ LORD, the Sacred Name (*Yahweh*)
- ☐ The LORD My Banner (*Jehovah Nissi*)
- ☐ The LORD My Shepherd (*Jehovah Raah*)
- ☐ The LORD Is There (*Jehovah Shammah*)
- ☐ The LORD Our Righteousness (*Jehovah Tsidkenu*)

As we close today in prayer, let's have a fast from asking. Let's simply enjoy a few moments standing (or sitting, or kneeling) in a prayer of adoration, awe, and wonder before God. I will begin and then you can take over the prayer. Simply tell Him your favorite seven things about Him, and tell Him each name you know for Him and why you know that name is a good, true, and right name.

You are going to close the prayer today as well. I wish I could be with you for this; we would have an adoration fest. You might have a tendency to begin praying silently as this is going to be very personal. Please don't let yourself do that. Giving voice to prayers of adoration will lift your spirit and excite your heart and mind.

When Jesus entered Jerusalem for the final time before going to the cross, the people shouted praises to Him: "Hosanna to the Son of David! Blessed is He who comes in the name of the Lord, even the King of Israel! Hosanna in the Highest!"[17]

When questioned about the people's praises, Jesus responded that if the people remained silent, the rocks would cry out praises.[18] Let's not forfeit our praises to the rocks.

CLOSING PRAYER

"Father of lights, my Father in heaven, holy is Your name. Every generous act and every perfect gift come from You. In You there is not variation or shadow cast by turning. You are a solid rock and strong foundation. You do not change or shift as sand but are the same from everlasting to everlasting. I stand in awe of You, all You are, and all You have done in my life.
[*Share your WOWs with Him and tell Him your favorite names for Him. Close when you are ready. I will join you in your amen.*]
Amen."[19]

"Not only does sin hinder prayer; prayer hinders sin. The two are always opposed. The more careless we are about sin, the less we will pray. The more we pray, the less careless we will be about sin. Bothe are powerful forces. Which one is moving you?"
DR. ALVIN VANDER GRIEND.

"Thou has made us for Thyself, O Lord, and our heart is restless until it finds its rest in Thee."
ST. AUGUSTINE

Week Three

WEEK 3: CONFESSION, DAY

DAY 1

Week 3: Confession

OPENING PRAYER

"Father, You are the God of Truth. Your Son is the Word of Truth and Your Holy Spirit is the Spirit of Truth. Truth resides with and in You alone. Open my eyes that I might see truth, my mind that I might know truth, and my heart that I might receive truth. Correct my crooked understanding and make it straight. Thank You, Father, that as I grow in relationship with You, I grow in truth. Teach me to abide more fully in truth. Your love is truth. Teach me to abide more fully in Your love. In Jesus' name, amen."[1]

SWEET CONFESSIONS

The book *The Confessions* by St. Augustine helped me to better understand confession in prayer. Like many, I believed confession to consist of a spiritually self-berating prayer wherein one admits to God the profoundly wretched state of one's thoughts and actions. This was the period in prayer, I thought, in which a person would enter a moment of humility before God, crawling on the knees spiritually, if you will, begging acceptance and forgiveness, and hoping to receive them if the confession was genuine and convincing enough. Confession served as an emotional purge, a moment to get off one's chest what had been causing turmoil and discomfort to the conscience. Yet, only hours or days later, the undesirable behavior gets repeated. Can you relate?

The principle and purpose of confession can be easily twisted. Several years back I talked with a youth pastor who led a group of college students. He was frustrated with a similar false teaching that had taken hold, not only in that group but among many of their generation: a belief that because forgiveness covers all sin, any sin is permissible as long as one asks forgiveness afterward.

Consequently, anyone could blatantly persist in sin as long as they confessed the sin in prayer and asked forgiveness. Partying, sleeping around, cheating on exams, lying to parents, and the like were to be expected, so the teaching went, because they were youth after all. In order to be Christian, they needed

MY VOICE, HIS HEART

only to confess their sinful activities in prayer and ask forgiveness following the objectionable activities and all would be right. Have you been there or known someone who has taken this view of sin, confession, and forgiveness?

I have a third incorrect view of confession for you. If you have not related to the first two, maybe this one will hit home. It says that confession in prayer is only necessary for those who have really sinned big time. Possibly it is necessary once in a while for the rest of us, who have inadvertently racked up a number of smaller sins and need to make sure we don't have too much unforgiven sin separating us from God, making Him more mad than glad with us. Confession in this case becomes necessary to wipe off the sin scale so mercy and forgiveness, rather than condemnation, will once again tip in our favor. I have been here as well. Have you?

What is your view of confession?

_____

_____

_____

_____

How often do you have a time of confession in prayer?

☐ Every day   ☐ Occasionally   ☐ Rarely   ☐ Only When Needed

Confession in prayer is not what most of us would deem as sweet. Yet, friend, it is exactly that. This most misunderstood aspect of prayer has become the most powerful for me. The three above views of confession miss the mark, some more entirely than others.

In an effort to untangle and straighten our understanding of this important principle, we are going to first look at another aspect of prayer that is often intertwined with confession: repentance. Scripture does not confuse these two principles, yet somehow we have.

The Old and New Testaments use entirely different words for repentance

WEEK 3: CONFESSION, DAY 1

and confession. The word used for repent or repentance appears 75 times in scripture. It appears in almost one third of the books in the Old Testament and almost half the books in the New Testament. This is a good indication to us that repentance is an important principle God wants us to understand and incorporate in our lives.

In the Old Testament, the Hebrew word translated as repent or repentance is *shuwb*. The meaning gives us incredible insight into the heart of repentance. *Shuwb* means "to turn back, return; to return unto, go back or come back."

Now prepare yourself for what we find in the New Testament. The word used here is *metanoeo*, which means "to change one's mind, to think differently, to change one's mind for better, heartily to amend with abhorrence of one's past sins."

If you are up for it, grab your Bible and go to Ephesians 4:17-24. Pay special attention to the last two verses. Write them here:

Ephesians 4:23-24

"
_____

_____

_____

_____."

Can you see? Repentance is not an emotional purge or an instance of feeling sorry. It is not a momentary acknowledgement of wrong-doing. Repentance is a complete mind change, a renewal of the mind in the likeness and righteousness of God. Repentance is not a backwards glance or even a good long look over one's shoulder to examine past sin, but a complete turning of one's mind, body, and spirit away from sin and one's former ways and toward God and His ways.

Like me, you may be thinking, "I thought that's what confession was. Then what is confession?" I'm glad you asked, friend.

MY VOICE, HIS HEART

The Hebrew word for confess or confession used in the Old Testament is *yadah*. It appears 114 times. I cannot help but smile as I write this. *Yadah* is primarily translated as "praise, give thanks, thank, thanksgiving, and thankful." It is used 93 times this way. For the remaining occurrences, it is translated as "confess, make confession."

The New Testament is going to help us gain a fuller picture of confession. The Greek word used here is *homologeo*. Its literal translation is "same word" and it means, "to say the same thing as another, to agree with; to concede, declare or confess; to profess, to declare openly, speak out freely; to praise or celebrate."

To confess, then, is to say the same thing God says. Confession is to agree with God, concede that His way is the right way, and to openly declare it and speak it out freely. To agree with God is to agree in truth. God is Truth. Jesus is the Word of Truth. The Holy Spirit is the Spirit of Truth. When we agree with God, we align ourselves with truth. Confession is the declaration of truth in prayer.

This is why confession can also be translated as "praise, give thanks, thank, thanksgiving, thankful." When we are declaring truth, that God is love and mercy and grace, for example, our hearts are full of praise and thankfulness for this truth.

The principle of confession has become increasingly important as the modern, progressive teaching that "every person has their own truth and needs only follow their heart to discover that truth" has darkened the hearts and minds of generations. Scripture teaches us that "The heart is deceitful above all things."[2] Following one's heart may sound like insightful wisdom but it is foolish deception.

Confession that aligns our spirit with the Spirit of Truth, that declares the Word of Truth over our life and circumstances, and concedes all to the God of Truth, brings light and life into dark and dead places. God tells us that His Word "is alive and powerful and is sharper than any two-edged sword, cutting between soul and spirit, between joint and marrow. It exposes our inner most thoughts and desires."[3] Let's be eager for God to expose our inner most to His light of love and truth.

WEEK 3: CONFESSION, DAY 1

How then do confession and repentance work together? Confession with repentance is substantive, transformative, and healing. Confession without repentance is hollow. While confession takes place on the lips and acknowledges truth, repentance takes place in the heart and mind, conforming and reforming both to the truth. We can see the truth, know the truth, and declare the truth in confession; but we still must align our lives to the truth in repentance.

Aligning our lives to His truth requires turning away from our selfish desires. It requires turning away from the lies the world would have us believe, to the truth His love has revealed. It requires letting go of worldly treasures we have held onto so tightly, and turning to receive with open hands the eternal treasures He has for us. We must align our mind, spirit, and body to God's truth.

Friend, at moments this may require every bit of strength we have. God says we are to love Him with all our heart, all our soul, all our mind, and all our strength. He understands the challenge and He provides His love and liberating Spirit to get us there. "For it is God who is working in you, enabling you both to desire and to work out His good purpose."[4]

Are you prepared to let go of your definition of truth—how you believe your life should look, what the world says is right and important, what you have pursued in order to be happy and fulfilled? Are you prepared to embrace God's truth—His plans to prosper and grow you, what He says is right and worthwhile, what He says will bring you joy and an abundant life?

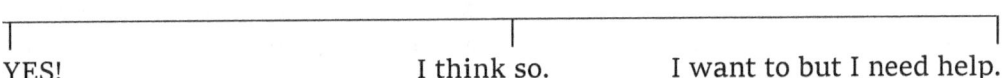

YES!   I think so.   I want to but I need help.

I am ready! I hope you are, too.

Read the following encouragement and assurance from Psalm 34:8 and Psalms 19:7-11. Underline or highlight any words that oppose and expose a lie you have previously believed.

> "Oh, taste and see that the LORD is good!"

MY VOICE, HIS HEART

"The law of the LORD is perfect, reviving the soul;
the testimony of the LORD is sure,
making wise the simple;
the precepts of the LORD are right,
rejoicing the heart;
the commandment of the LORD is pure, enlightening the eyes;
the fear of the LORD is clean, enduring forever;
the rules of the LORD are true,
and righteous altogether.
More to be desired are they than gold,
even much fine gold;
sweeter also than honey and drippings of the honeycomb.
Moreover, by them is your servant warned;
in keeping them there is great reward."

In closing our time together today, let's have a time of confession and repentance in prayer. We will begin by confessing the truth contained in the Psalms above. Notice the exclamations David used in his confessions. He spoke these truths out freely and openly. So can we!

If you have been misled into believing a lie that God's truth has now revealed to you, take the opportunity today to acknowledge that lie and turn fully to God's truth. As we confess His truth, it is like honey on our lips. As we turn our heart and mind away from lies and toward His truth, He revives our souls.

CLOSING PRAYER

"LORD, You are good and Your mercy endures forever. I praise You that You have revealed Your Truth to me, that I may know the truth and be set free by Your truth. While lies determine to shackle, bind, and destroy me, Your truth saves and revives me.

[*Give voice to the words from the Psalms above, confessing His truth and repenting from the specific lie(s) you choose to turn from today.*]

You, LORD, are my rescuer and the Savior of my life. Thank You for rescuing me from the lies of the enemy and saving me from my sin. Your love is greater than life. In the powerful name of my Savior Jesus Christ, I pray. Amen."[5]

WEEK 3: CONFESSION, DAY

DAY 2

Week 3: Confession

OPENING PRAYER

"LORD, my eyes are dull and I see poorly. My ears are obstructed, and my hearing is impeded. I desire to see clearly that I might see Your hand at work and join in. I desire to hear Your voice leading me as I meditate on Your word and learn to follow Your way for my life. Heal my sight, pull the cotton of the world from my ears and train them to hear Your voice. Teach me to walk in Your ways that I may know the fullness of Your love for me. In Jesus' name I pray. Amen."[6]

CONFESSION & REPENTANCE: A FURTHER CLARIFICATION

I would not be described as a passionate person, but I have to tell you, I am passionate about the discussion we are having now. I desperately want you to know and understand these two aspects of prayer, so much so that I have more notes on this than on any other section of this study. So hang in here with me. Don't let yourself become bored if you find me restating a thought. It is simply my attempt to clarify a principle that has been life changing for me and I believe can, at a minimum, be an "A-ha!" moment for you.

In simple terms, we can say confession acknowledges and proclaims the truth. Repentance rejects and turns away from the lie, and turns towards and embraces the truth. Both are needed. God never reveals truth simply for us to gain knowledge. Truth always has a work to complete in us. God's truth will never return to Him void or empty.[7] If we do not allow truth to do its work in us, it will indeed do its work in another while we willfully remain in the darkness of deception.

Before we go further, I have six summary statements for us so far. Would you mark the statements that make sense? I hope you are able to check them all, but if not, that's okay. We still have over three weeks together and God is a better communicator than I am. He will teach you even deeper truths than I can ever hope to.

MY VOICE, HIS HEART

- ☐ Confession acknowledges and proclaims God's Word is The Truth.
- ☐ Confession acknowledges a lie as a lie.
- ☐ Confession acknowledges where one's will, actions, thoughts, and desires have lined up with God's truth (obedience).
- ☐ Confession acknowledges where one's will, actions, thoughts, and desires have lined up with a lie and have opposed God's truth (disobedience).
- ☐ Repentance rejects and turns away from the lie and turns toward the truth, embracing the God of Truth.
- ☐ Repentance turns from a place of disobedience to a place of obedience in one's will, actions, thoughts, and desires.

LOVE THAT BINDS US AND LIES THAT BLIND US

In Week 1 of our time together, we saw in the book of Genesis Adam and God walking in unbroken relationship, in one will, in truth, and in love—until Adam believed two lies. Adam accepted the lie that God was withholding greater knowledge from him—and the principle that went along with this, that he would be more powerful or more equal to God if he possessed that greater knowledge.

The second lie Adam believed is this: that God had lied to him about death, the consequence of disobedience. God told Adam that if he ate the fruit from the tree of the knowledge of good and evil, he would die. The enemy lied and told Adam that he surely would not die. Despite everything Adam knew about God, when Adam aligned his thoughts, will, actions, and desires to the lies instead of God's truth, the darkness of sin resulted in a broken relationship. When God approached Adam, he would neither confess nor repent. Instead he blamed another person, Eve.

I can relate. Can you? Have you ever blamed someone else for your sin?

- ☐ Thank heavens, no.
- ☐ Once, and never again.
- ☐ Unfortunately, many times.
- ☐ Probably more than I realize.

WEEK 3: CONFESSION, DAY 2

If you are willing, would you share about it here? _____

_____

_____

_____

If we blame someone else for our disobedience and sin, the guilt of sin remains and consequently the penalty of sin remains. Through blame, we are simply attempting to shift the guilt and ultimate penalty elsewhere. The penalty of sin is death. Death is a destructive foe that will ultimately take everything we have, including our life. We do not want to toss it around like a hot potato, for it will scorch and burn everything it touches. We must extinguish death's influence in our lives. Only One person has defeated death, and He has offered that victory to us freely: "For the wages of sin is death, but the free gift of God is eternal life in Christ Jesus our Lord."[8]

Confession and repentance bring God's forgiveness. Forgiveness means no more guilt, no more blame, no more penalty, and no more death. My spirit just shouted, "Hallelujah!" Why would we ever again attempt to blame others or shift guilt?

Let's be quick to go to God with our sin. Let's delight in confession. Let's abhor the sin and embrace God in repentance. We are not meant to live in the misery and shackles of sin. We are not meant to return to it, like a dog returns to his own vomit. We are not meant to live blinded by sin, stumbling in the darkness. God made us to live in fullness of life with Him. God saves, God forgives, and God redeems. He makes all things new! May we turn from sin and embrace Him every day.

Before we close in prayer today, we are going to be quiet before God. There are likely areas in our life—in our will, actions, thoughts, and desires—that need His loving attention and forgiveness. I am going to open my prayer journal and record everything He would prompt me to address with Him in prayer as we close today.

I am not going to share what He prompts in me, and, if you are doing this in a group, you do not have to share what He is asking you to address. Let's spend five or so minutes quietly before Him—or take as long as you need. Then we will close in a prayer of confession and repentance.

_____
_____
_____
_____
_____

CLOSING PRAYER

"Father, You do not stand in judgement but You reach down from heaven to save. The enemy accuses day and night, but You, O LORD, forgive. You alone have the power to redeem my life from the pit.

My God is the Everlasting God. He is the LORD Who Heals. He is the Wonderful Counselor and Prince of Peace. His ways are righteous. He makes streams in the desert. All creation declares His glory.

Father, I desire to know You more intimately, to have an unbroken relationship with You. Yet I have sinned against You in thought, word, and deed. My will has been my own and my heart has been far from You. Forgive my sins...

[Share personally with God what He has prompted in your spirit for confession and repentance.]

Thank You, Father, for the forgiveness You offer through the sacrifice of Your Son Jesus Christ. Thank You that He alone paid the penalty of death for my sin. Thank You for the power of His resurrection to new life that You have made possible for me.

You have offered to pour out Your Spirit to all who turn from their sin and accept Christ as LORD and Savior. I turn from my sin and I accept Jesus as my LORD and Savior. I ask for Your Holy Spirit to dwell in me.

WEEK 3: CONFESSION, DAY 2

Thank You, Father, for holding no record of my many wrongs against You. Take joy, LORD, in this dusty, broken vessel that You lovingly make into Your dwelling place. Clean and purify Your temple as only You can. Lead me in Your way everlasting. Amen."[9]

WEEK 3: CONFESSION, DAY

DAY 3

Week 3: Confession

OPENING PRAYER

"Father, You have not left me in the dark, but have given me the light of truth. Spread this light throughout my spirit that I would be full of light, that my life will shine with the truth of Your love, Your goodness, and Your mercy. In the name of Jesus, Who is the way, the truth, and the life, I pray. Amen."[10]

THE TRUTH GOD REVEALS

I must tell you, yesterday did not go as expected. I had not intended on closing the way we did. I had to run to the bathroom for tissue, and, as I am using a room at my church to complete this study, I was hoping my pastor would not come in to check on me. I wanted time alone with God; and, to have my pastor walk in and find me with snot hanging out of my nose is not my idea of fun. Apparently, I needed yesterday's study and time with my Heavenly Father more than I thought. I hope you did as well.

As we looked at "Love that Binds Us and Lies that Blind Us" in our time together yesterday, we went back to Genesis and considered the approach the enemy took in deceiving and lying to Adam. The enemy of our soul takes the same approach with us today that he took with Adam in the garden. Lies from the enemy generally take two forms:

1. The enemy tries to convince us that the world's truth is better than God's truth, that it is more enlightening. He makes false claims that we will ultimately become more like God—more knowledgeable, more loving, more powerful—if we believe the world's truth rather than God's truth.

2. The enemy tries to convince us that God has lied to us, mislead us, or been unclear with us, or that we somehow misunderstood the words He has told us; and that if we will simply accept the lie the world is selling, the consequences God has told us we would experience, will not actually befall us.

MY VOICE, HIS HEART

Do you recognize these approaches? What lies does the world attempt to sell us as truth?

_____
_____
_____
_____
_____
_____

What lies has the enemy attempted to convince you personally of?

_____
_____
_____
_____
_____
_____

The enemy is cunning. Joseph Goebbels, the Minister of Propaganda for Nazi Germany and one of Hitler's closest associates, is credited with single-handedly presenting a favorable image of the Third Reich Nazi Regime to the German people. The shrewdly effective method Goebbels employed was stunningly simple: accuse the enemy of what you yourself are doing. Satan came up with this method long before Goebbels ever did. He used it in the garden with Adam, accusing God of lying to Adam, when in fact Satan himself is the father of lies.[11]

WEEK 3: CONFESSION, DAY 3

WHAT BINDS YOUR HEART?

Are you bound by the truth of love, hope, peace, purpose, and joy that God offers? Or are you bound by lies of rejection, shame, worthlessness, anxiety, and loneliness? I love the hymn "Come, Thou Fount of Every Blessing," which asks God to use His grace as a fetter to bind my wandering heart to His. The promises of the world are convincing. The deception of the enemy is cunning. Abiding in God takes courage, mental alertness, and perseverance. But oh, how it is worth the effort! If love binds our heart, our heart overflows. If lies bind our heart, we are suffocated and strangled.

We have established that knowing and confessing the truth is not enough. We must turn from lies and disobedience and embrace the God of Truth. I want to share with you where the Bible clearly highlights this principle. Two places in scripture give an account of demons proclaiming the truth that Christ is the Son of God.[12] If demons know the truth and declare the truth, why are they not saved? The answer is simple, and it is chilling. They are not saved because they have rejected the truth. May we never reject a truth that God, in His goodness and mercy, reveals to us!

Friend, we need to embrace truth and reject lies. When our life, our thoughts, and our will are out of alignment with God, it is often because we have accepted one or more lies as true. When God reveals the truth to us, let us be quick to embrace it and reject the lie for good.

Romans 1:25 reads, "They exchanged the truth of God for a lie."

It is healthy and good to examine ourselves and ask what truths we may have exchanged for lies. On the following page, we are going to consider seven truths that God's Word establishes about you and me.

Then we are going to identify the lie that the world attempts to replace each truth with. Let's be honest about any lies we may be currently accepting.

MY VOICE, HIS HEART

Look up each scripture and draw a **straight** line from the scripture to the truth God reveals in that scripture.

Then draw a **wavy** line from the scripture to the lie the enemy poses against it.

Next, put a **checkmark** next to any lie that may have a foothold in your heart and mind.

Finally, **circle** the truth that God's Word speaks against that lie.

God's Goodness

Truth	Scripture	Lie
God created all things, and all of creation is held together in Him.	Jeremiah 29:11	My life is pointless and no one cares what happens to me.
God has a plan for my life and desires good things for me.	Colossians 1:16-17	God is just a feel-good, made-up figment of imagination. This world is here by happenstance.
God is a loving Father Who listens and cares for me personally.	Psalm 139:14-15	God is not interested in me personally. He doesn't take time to listen to me.
God designed me wonderfully and purposefully.	Matthew 6:6 & 2 Corinthians 6:18	I am an accident, a freak of nature. My body and the way I look aren't good enough.

WEEK 3: CONFESSION, DAY 3

My Identity

Truth	Scripture	Lie
God accepts me and I am completely and fully loved by Him.	Romans 5:8 Ephesians 3: 17-19	I cannot escape fear and anxiety. I will never have peace.
There is nothing I have to fear.	John 15:16 Ephesians 1:4-5	I have done too many bad things for God to want me; I have to be successful to be good enough for Him to love me.
I am chosen and adopted by God. I am His daughter.	2 Timothy 1:7 Isaiah 26:3 Philippians 4:6-7	I am a reject. I am abandoned and on my own. No one wants me.

The straight line is firm and reliable, just like God's truth. The wavy line is like shifting sand, just like the enemy's lies. Which will you choose to build your life on?

If you checked any of the lies, you now have the truth of God's Word to proclaim against them. If there is a truth I need to be reminded of repeatedly, I write in on a sticky note and post it somewhere I will see it often (my bathroom, my car, my bedside table) so I can begin to turn my thoughts to the truth and allow the meditations of my mind to become the meditations of my heart.[13] I also enjoy confessing these truths in prayer, asking God to increase my understanding of the scriptures and use them as a lamp to my feet and a light to my path.[14]

Well done, friend, this was a lot of work today. We will be referring back to everything we learned here. This is a fabulous investment of time in so many ways.

Let's close with a short prayer. Take a deep breath, slow your thoughts, and exhale.

MY VOICE, HIS HEART

CLOSING PRAYER

"Father, Your Word is light. Your Son is the light of the world. You have called us children of light. You have said we are to be light in this world. You have made it possible through Your Holy Spirit, Who lights up the darkness. God, by Your Holy Spirit, prompt me to quickly turn from the darkness of every lie and sin. Protect me and keep me from it. Ignite a fire in me for Your truth, so that nothing else will do.

In Jesus' name, I reject the lies I have allowed in my life.
[*Voice every lie you put a star next to in today's exercise.*]
I accept and abide in the truth You have shown me.
[*Voice every truth you circled.*]
I thank You, Father, and praise You in Jesus' name.
Amen." [15]

WEEK 3: CONFESSION, DAY

DAY 4

Week 3: Confession

OPENING PRAYER

"LORD, You are faithful and true. I am excited to be with You today. I thank You that even when I am not thinking of You, You are thinking of me. You even know the number of hairs on my head. I cannot imagine the patience required to count them all, yet patience is the calling card of Your loving-kindness toward me. Forgive me, Father, for my lack of patience. Forgive me for being quick to embrace enticing lies when patient thoughtfulness would have revealed Your truth. Quicken my spirit to Your truth, that I would turn toward truth and be repulsed by lies. In Jesus' name, amen."[16]

TURNING TOWARD LOVE: UNDERSTANDING SACRIFICE

My three beautiful daughters, how I love them! They have taught me the invaluable lesson of self-sacrifice…and goodness, how very thoroughly they have taught it. My oldest might even declare that it was her pleasure to be of service in such a way. My youngest, with a wily grin and mischievous squint, might say God had called her to the task and she obediently responded for the past 16 years. I imagine my middle daughter would ignore the silly comments, hug me good-bye, and be off to jump horses over heights that turn this momma's stomach inside out.

Love without self-sacrifice is not love at all.[17] God teaches us this principle from Genesis to Revelation. The single most quoted verse in all of scripture, John 3:16, summarizes the extreme lengths of God's love by the sacrifice He was willing to make. "For God so loved the world that He gave His only Son…"

Can you imagine that kind of love? I have three daughters and I would not give any of them up, let alone turn one of them over, knowing her death was imminent. Who did God love so much that He would be willing to make this level of sacrifice?

MY VOICE, HIS HEART

John 3:16 tells us, "...that whosoever believes in Him would not perish but have everlasting life." You and I are the "whosoever" God loves so completely that He would make this unthinkable personal sacrifice in order to have a forever relationship with us. Most days I don't even know what to do with this. It is beyond my ability to fathom.

The apostle Paul speaks of the length and width, and the height and depth, of God's love that surpasses all knowledge and understanding.[18] He encourages us to know in the depths of our spirit that nothing, no nothing, can separate us ever, no never, from God's love.[19] I agree with King David when he declares that "Such knowledge is too wonderful for me, too great for me to understand!"[20] Friend, I pray that while the depths, fullness, and faithfulness of God's love for us may be too great for us to understand, we will never stop pressing in to know and experience it more.

As we saw in our scripture activity yesterday, God's love accepts us right where we are. How grateful I am that He does not leave us where He finds us, but begins a beautiful work in us that reveals His true bride in all her glory. Pop culture or Oprah magazine might tell us to aspire to become the best version of ourself; but friend, in God's hands we are not just the next reworked 2.0 upgrade that will be replaced, obsolete, or out of style next season. In God's hands we are eternal creatures who become increasingly full of light, brilliant to behold, a source of truth, love, and goodness.

He asks us to sacrifice our *self* in exchange for Himself. Our *self* may include much that we deem incredibly worthwhile right now. If there's something I'm struggling to let go of, something I believe God is asking me to sacrifice, it helps when I do three things.

1. I consider whether I might be accepting a lie that is making the struggle more difficult. Is there a lie I believe that makes what I am holding onto seem more worthwhile or more valuable than it actually is? Is there a lie that makes me believe letting go of whatever it is, will be a detrimental loss?

2. I consider the true value or worth of the thing in question, in light of eternity. Is it truly of eternal value or worth, or is it only temporary and of passing value?

3. I consider who is the true owner of what I am holding onto. Is it my resource or possession, or is it God's?

WEEK 3: CONFESSION, DAY 4

By the time I get through these three deliberations, I have either cast the thing far from me and walked the other way, held my hand open while God gently takes it, or committed to letting it go and prayed for His help in not grabbing it back.

Is there anything you believe God is asking you to sacrifice, that you are struggling to let go of?

_____

_____

Here are a few examples of 'self' I have let go of as I have pursued God's will for my life over my own:

- Left an international career to pursue a healthy marriage and family.

- Let go of personal validation and value based on earnings and influence, and embraced my eternal value as a daughter of God.

- Stopped watching a favorite TV program and TV personality after acknowledging that what I justified as innocent, fun entertainment was actually feeding me a steady diet of lies.

- Redefined my beauty from being dependent on designer labels and spa treatments, to a beauty that is dependent on love, joy, hope and peace.

- Accepted that I do not own any of the money I have, but am merely a steward of a resource God has temporarily placed in my hands.

- Let go of the anger, bitterness, and arrogance of a life of comparison and competition with others; and embraced the intimate love God has for me and others individually.

THE JOY OF SACRIFICE

While I have struggled in some areas, the majority of everything I have sacrificed has been a joy and relatively easy. I would even, at times, say effortless, in the way a mother will gladly forgo her own way to engage in the joy of raising her children. Not a single picture she takes will be to capture a moment of her sacrifice but to celebrate the joy right before her.

MY VOICE, HIS HEART

Speaking of pictures of joy and sacrifice, there is one important picture we have all likely seen, a picture God has painted with stunning detail through words in scripture. It is a picture He has prompted great artists to paint, sculpt, and construct throughout the centuries. A picture that hangs in great museums, churches and gathering places. It is the picture of Jesus Christ hanging on the cross. The one picture God captured of His Son doesn't seem to be the ideal family photo I would have chosen if I were God. Yet it is a picture of the most beautiful sacrifice ever made. Praise God that we have it. May we never discount it or forget it.

As a young believer I could never fathom how Jesus could actually choose to make the sacrifice He did. As God Himself, He could have easily refused death on the cross. He could have changed His mind at any point and ordered a legion of angels to intervene.[21] Why would He endure the mocking insults, the beatings, and the pain of it all?

I want to share a scripture with you that pierced me when I first came across it. Grab your Bible and turn to Hebrews 12:1-2. Will you write in CAPITAL letters the missing word?

"Let us run with endurance the race that is set before us, looking to Jesus, the founder and perfecter of our faith, who for the _____ that was set before Him endured the cross, despising the shame, and is seated at the right hand of the throne of God."

Now, lest you start to believe that the joy set before Jesus was the powerful position He knew He would go back to, sitting at the right hand of God, or the joy He experienced in completing the work the Father sent Him to complete, let me clarify.

The Father, Son and Holy Spirit are always in perfect love and perfect unity. Unity that never was, is, or ever will be broken. Jesus never lost His eternal position in Heaven. He never ceased being the Son. Returning to His position at the right hand of the Father was simply a matter of location. So, what was the joy set before Jesus that motivated Him to endure the cross?

Let's press deeper. The Greek word used here for joy is *chara*. It means "exceedingly joyful, cheerfulness, calm delight." And, are you ready for this?

WEEK 3: CONFESSION, DAY 4

The 59 times *chara* is used in the New Testament always refer to "the joy received from you; the cause or occasion of joy; of persons who are one's joy."

Jesus Christ is saying to us, to *you*, "You are my joy."

Write your name in the space below and allow Him to speak the words directly to you as you acknowledge this breathtaking truth.

"You, _____, are my joy."

This pierces me still. Let nothing convince us otherwise.

The relationship we have with Jesus is meant to be full and running over with joy. Christians are meant to be the most joy-filled people on earth. No, we are not meant to be raving lunatics, running around with our hands in the air, a perma-grin on our faces, singing praise songs, and blessing everyone in sight (not that there is anything wrong with this). Sometimes our *chara* may be *exceedingly joyful*. Sometimes it may be *cheerfulness*. Sometimes, it may simply be a *calm delight*.

Which expression of joy most appeals to you?

☐ Exceedingly joyful   ☐ Cheerfulness   ☐ Calm delight

Jesus' heart overflows with all of these when He looks at you and thinks of you. Do you believe it?

☐ Yes, praise God

☐ I am trying but it seems too good to be true

☐ Lord, help me to believe

We must do something a little difficult now. We must come full circle on this so we can better understand what joy and sacrifice have to do with confession and repentance. We are, after all, learning about confession and repentance this week.

MY VOICE, HIS HEART

There is joy in sacrifice. Not only for Jesus but for us as well. Confession and repentance are sacrifices. Sometimes easy, even effortless, sacrifices. But at other times, they are almost unbearable sacrifices that require wrestling and soul searching. In repentance, when we acknowledge the lies we have held onto, God tells us to let go of and turn away from them. We must sacrifice the lie, if you will. We have to sacrifice our version of the truth or a belief we've held tightly onto. When we acknowledge disobedience and turn away from it, we are sacrificing our will, desires, thoughts, and actions, and embracing God's will. Repentance is sacrificing *self* and turning to God.

If we will first press into the love and goodness of God during confession, we will find that the joy set before us in our relationship with our Heavenly Father will enable us in repentance to sacrifice whatever aspect of self He has shown us needs to go.

Thank you so much, friend, for sticking with me today. I long to have a discussion with you around everything we have covered and how God is working in your heart and mind. I know you have insights to share that I have never thought of. If you are doing this study as part of a group, please be generous with your insights and share what God is teaching you.

INTERACTIVE PRAYER DOWNLOAD

If you are incorporating the Let's Pray Today Ministries "Prayer for Beginners" MP3 downloads with this study, I am going to let my dear friend Sylvia close in prayer with you today. Please go to Prayer #2 on track 3. Listen and pray all the way through to the end (approx. 7 minutes).

You may use that as your closing prayer for today, or the following concluding prayer. Please remember to share with God in prayer anything you are struggling to let go of that He is gently asking you to place in His hands.

"Father God, how can it be that I am Your joy? How can it be that You delight in me? How is this breathtaking truth possible? It is too wonderful for me to understand. I am made of dust, yet You value me. You have created me for eternity. My sight is dim, my mind is weak, and my spirit stumbles about. Yet You show me great things, You give wisdom

WEEK 3: CONFESSION, DAY 4

generously, and You strengthen my spirit and straighten my path. There is nothing worth more than You. There is nothing worth being separated from You. Please show me what I am holding onto that is detestable to You or that is not mine to hold onto.
[*Share personally with God what you believe He is asking you to let go of.*]
Thank You, Father, for Your gentleness, truth, and love. In Jesus' name I let go of what You ask me to sacrifice. In its place I receive Your goodness and joy. Amen."[22]

WEEK 3: CONFESSION, DAY

DAY 5

Week 3: Confession

"LORD, today open my heart to the truth—to recognize it and comprehend it. Help me as I learn to distinguish Your truth from the lies I inadvertently tell myself. Teach me as I courageously turn from those lies to live each day in the truth of Your Word. I praise You and I thank You for Your guidance and for the power of Your Holy Spirit, Who lives in me and enables me to do Your will. Amen"[23]

NOTHING IS BETTER THAN GOD

A truth can become a lie when we take the focus off of God and put it where it does not belong. While you and I are pressing into the depths of God's love, the world is pressing into the depths of darkness. While we can see the truth that nothing is better than God, the world will do everything possible to convince us that believing in "nothing" is better than believing in God. The fruits of embracing nothing are hopelessness, loneliness, worthlessness, and despair. Scripture tells us that the fruit of embracing God is love, joy, peace, patience, goodness, kindness, gentleness, and self-control. The world can never enjoy the fruits of God by embracing nothing. No matter how hard it tries, it is simply impossible. Whatever we embrace tends to embrace us in return. An embrace can quickly become a secure binding that restricts or influences our behaviors and thoughts.

- If we are bound by lies, we are bound to lie (to ourselves and to others).
- If we are bound by love, we are bound to love (generously, compassionately, and selflessly).
- If we are bound by truth, we are bound to abide in truth (in our heart, mind, and spirit).

On the following page is a chart to complete as you continue in this study.

MY VOICE, HIS HEART

- Anytime God reveals a lie to you, especially one you have held onto tightly, I would ask you to write it down under LIE.
- Then, record the truth God used to reveal the lie to you under TRUTH.
- Finally, anchor the truth with its location in scripture.

Begin by writing in a lie you identified on Day 3 this week. When you fill this chart up, grab your journal and continue there.

If you have a hard time finding a specific scripture, you might try searching on biblegateway.com. Or, open to the back of your Bible and use the concordance. If these both fail, ask a pastor or someone you know who regularly engages in Bible study. They will likely be able to help you find a scripture that will become incredibly dear to you.

TRUTH	SCRIPTURE	LIE

WEEK 3: CONFESSION, DAY 5

REFRESHED, REVIVED & RESTORED

God laments in Isaiah 29:13, "...they honor me with their lips but their hearts are far from me." In Matthew 15:8 Jesus applies this same scripture to the religious leaders of His day. May God never say this about us. May His grace like a fetter bind our hearts to His. Let us never forgo confession and repentance in prayer. Lips that praise amidst an unrepentant heart are like a clanging symbol to God's ears.[24]

This is my encouragement and promise to you this week. "Repent, then, and turn to God, so that your sins may be wiped out, that times of refreshing may come from the Lord."[25] Confession and repentance will not only restore us to a right relationship with God, but they will revive our heart and refresh our spirit.

Would you please close us in prayer today? Write out your prayer and then pray it out loud. If you are doing this study in a group, grab hold of the confidence that is ours in Christ and close your group time voicing the prayer you write out below.

CLOSING PRAYER

"Heavenly Father, _____

_____

_____

_____

_____

_____

_____

_____ Amen."

"The key to thankfulness is not to view God through the lens of our circumstances, but to view our circumstances through the lens of God's love and sovereign purpose."
ANNE GRAHAM LOTZ

"Blessed is she who has believed that the Lord would fulfill His promises to her!"
LUKE 1:45 (NIV)

Week Four

WEEK 4: THANKSGIVING, DAY

DAY 1

Week 4: Thanksgiving

"All who call on the name of the Lord will be saved. You have given this promise Father. You have not withheld Your salvation from me but have revealed what was kept hidden for generations. There is no other name under heaven by which men can be saved, but by the name of Jesus Christ. Thank You, Father, for Your Son. In His powerful name I pray. Amen."[1]

THE PESSIMIST, THE OPTIMIST & THE PSALMIST

In my teen years, I briefly worked with a woman who always seemed to have a smile plastered across her face. It nauseated me. *What a big fake*, I thought. *Life is hard; no one is always happy.* I doubted that anyone could possess joy and thankfulness as a matter of daily life. I believed these attributes could mark the majority of one's life at best but not all of one's life.

As a young adult, I accepted the pessimist-versus-optimist personality profiles. I believed people simply had a certain pre-programmed propensity for looking at the same set of circumstances from either a positive perspective or a negative bent. When life was difficult, the optimist would sail through it by focusing on the potential opportunity any given difficulty might yield.

The optimist would be able to maintain an eternal state of blissful positivity simply by donning rose-colored glasses in all demanding situations. The pessimist, on the other hand, was forever fated to be stripped of happiness and handicapped with a doom and gloom outlook. For her, happiness would always be fleeting and ethereal at best. People were forced to accept what they were—or so I thought.

The less-emotionally driven few, I believed, could look at circumstances from a realistic perspective, handicapped by neither a false sense of optimism nor pessimism in their assessments. The realist could determine appropriate

MY VOICE, HIS HEART

levels of utter happiness, cautious concern, or anxious dread in light of the conditions and happenings of any given set of events.

I, of course, considered myself in this latter group. I believed I possessed clear-headed logic which would save me from either extreme of optimism or pessimism. In my mind, I was unhindered by the emotional nonsense which hampers a true and unaffected understanding.

Are you cringing at my arrogance? I am cringing right along with you, I assure you. I had so blindly accepted worldly wisdom and a sense of intellectual superiority, I was in desperate need of Godly wisdom.

Throughout the Psalms and repeatedly in the lives of the prophets (Isaiah, Jeremiah, and Daniel come to mind especially as my favorites), we see perspectives change depending on, not a preprogrammed personality or even how one views one's circumstances, but rather *where* one is looking when viewing one's circumstances.

When my eyes are set on myself, my ability to handle successfully any given situation will determine my positive or negative perception of the circumstances. The more self-confident I am, the more optimistic will be my outlook. If my self-esteem is low, my outlook will be more pessimistic.

Past failures or successes will feed into this sense of either low self-esteem or strong self-confidence. If I feel equipped to handle the situation coming at me, I will have a sense of calm or even excitement over the challenge. If I feel ill-equipped, a sense of overwhelming hesitation, fear or panic may grip my heart. If my eyes are on me alone, the quality of person I see myself to be will depend only on outside circumstances and on whether I succeed or fail in dealing with them.

When my eyes are set on the world, circumstances seem bigger and bolder and I simply become a point of response or reaction to the events of the world. Wonderful events produce happiness and elation, while worrisome events produce anxiety and unrest. The portrayal of events in the evening news will determine how restful or fitful my sleep becomes. Who is elected to which office will send me into a state of either anxiety or elation. If my eyes are set on the world, I feel almost no control over what happens to me or those around me. I become powerless to effect true change.

WEEK 4: THANKSGIVING, DAY 1

Yet, when my eyes are set on God, His ability to effectively handle and be successful amidst any given situation produces a calm assurance in my heart and mind, even when I have a personal failure.

As well, recalling God's past faithfulness further bolsters my faith and assurance. Worldly events are seen in the light of eternity, subject to God's plan and sovereignty. Goodness is to be celebrated and enjoyed. Evil is to be departed from, overcome, defeated, and destroyed...but never, ever feared. I am able to see myself rightly as a powerful daughter of God who is purposed to step into such a time as this and impact the people and events in my area of influence and beyond.

The focus of our eyes will determine our perspective. Our perspective will determine our response. Like the Psalmists, we must keep our eyes fixed on God.

Complete the following Psalms by filling in the missing word.

"But my _____ are fixed on you, Sovereign LORD; in you I take refuge—do not give me over to death." Psalm 141:8 (NIV)

"My _____ are ever on the LORD, for only He will release my feet from the snare." Psalm 25:15 (NIV)

"To you I lift up my _____, to you who are enthroned in heaven." Psalm 123:1 (NIV)

"I keep my _____ always on the LORD. With Him at my right hand, I will not be shaken." Psalm 16:8 (NIV)

Why do I talk about any of this? What does the focus of our eyes, our perspective, and our response have to do with thanksgiving and prayer? Perfect question. These are all important because God calls us to do the impossible in one particular area of our life and we cannot do it without addressing these first.

MY VOICE, HIS HEART

Grab your Bible again, turn to 1 Thessalonians 5:18 and write it on the next page. You might also highlight verses 16 and 17, but for this study today we are going to focus on verse 18.

"
_____

_____

_____

_____."

Welcome to a key principle I struggled with for years. God calls us to do the impossible. He calls us to respond with thanksgiving in every circumstance of life.

The apostle Paul demonstrated for us a life that did exactly this. While in prison, in chains, beaten and hungry, Paul again and again gives thanks, even to the extent of overflowing with songs of praise to God. We see this in Acts 16:25, Philippians 1, Colossians 1:3-12, and Ephesians 5:20. How can we possibly hope to respond like Paul, or take the advice of James and "count it all joy when [we] meet trials of various kinds"?[2]

Throughout the Psalms (for examples, see Psalms 100, 136 & 138), David recognizes that all has been given by God's hand and gives thanks to God in times of success and in time of failure, in times of abundance and in times of poverty, in times of lighthearted cheer and in times of deep struggle.

God exchanges beauty for ashes, joy for mourning, and praise for despair.[3] When we are sitting in the misery of the ashes and cannot imagine that any beauty can come from it, we must take our eyes off of the ashes and refocus them where they are meant to be fixed: on our loving, almighty, attentive, Heavenly Father Who delights in redeeming the worst of sinners and the worst of circumstances. Only then is the impossible, possible. Only then can thanksgiving flow from a broken, overwhelmed heart.

If we will commit to this shift in our focus, we will find that our hardest trials may become our greatest source of joy and thanksgiving. In Day 5 we will

WEEK 4: THANKSGIVING, DAY 1

meet someone whose greatest struggle becomes a source of thanksgiving. I have seen God redeem horrible experiences to such a glorious degree that His children end up joyously thanking Him for circumstances and experiences which they had previously abhorred: cancer, troubled childhood, drug addiction, betrayal, and loss. God can redeem anything and everything. He will work it all out for our good and His glory.[4] We can trust Him and give thanks amidst every unwanted circumstance.

As you look back over this last year or the last decade, is there anything you are thankful for now that you were not thankful for while you were going through it? This may take some thought but is worth it.

_____

_____

_____

_____

Dear friend, you and I must stop giving thanks only for good things in prayer. As we begin to press in and learn all we can here, I hope you will see that the good things that happen to us only scratch the surface of all we have to be thankful for before God.

If we were to stop at this moment and you were to spend as much time as you needed expressing thanksgiving to God, how long would it take for you to share with Him everything for which you are thankful right now?

☐ 5 minutes tops
☐ A couple of hours
☐ Hmm, let me think about it
☐ All day and then some

The entire heart of thanksgiving is simply this: set your eyes on God, and not on self or the things of this world. I pray that as we begin to train our eyes to focus where they focus best, He will correct our perspective, and our response will be to overflow with thanksgiving. He is going to transform us. I hope you are ready.

MY VOICE, HIS HEART

INTERACTIVE PRAYER DOWNLOAD

If you are using the Let's Pray Today Ministries "Prayer for Beginners" mp3 download, go to Prayer #3 on Track 4. Listen and pray all the way through to the end of Prayer #3 (approx. 7 minutes). You may use that as your closing prayer, or join me below.

"Father, You are so good to me. Thank You for Your enduring love for me. Your name *El Roi* means God Who Sees. Thank You for seeing me. Thank You for the comfort of knowing that You always have Your eyes on me. Help me to keep my eyes always on You. Show me what I have not seen rightly. Correct my vision. Move my heart to thankfulness.

I thank You, LORD, for... [*share personally what you have written that you would like to thank God for*].

Thank You especially for Your Son Jesus and His life which He willingly gave for mine. In His Saving Name I pray. Amen."[5]

WEEK 4: THANKSGIVING, DAY

DAY 2

Week 4: Thanksgiving

OPENING PRAYER

"Gracious Father, thank You for the countless ways You provide for me. Thank You for the favor You have shown me. Thank You for the blessings You have poured out over me. Your thoughts outnumber the grains of sand. Thank You that in all those thoughts there is not one bad thought. Thank You that all Your thoughts for me are good and for my good. Your thoughts for me are for my growth, my welfare, and my future. O LORD, I desire to know You more fully, as I am fully known. I turn my eyes to You this day and fix my gaze rightly, that my heart would overflow with thankfulness in all circumstances. In Jesus' name I pray. Amen."[6]

WHAT IS THANKFULNESS?

Thankfulness has been described as an "attitude of gratitude." I have heard personality trainers claim that "attitude determines altitude," meaning that if we have a good attitude, we'll be able to overcome problems, attract others to us, and be more successful. As a parent, I have told my daughters on more than one occasion: "Go fix your attitude and come back when you're ready to be a positive contributor." Attitude is defined as "a settled way of thinking or feeling about someone or something, typically one that is reflected in a person's behavior."[7]

Our settled way of thinking about God will certainly impact how we respond to Him. However, having a positive view of God does not mean we will be appropriately thankful. Many agnostics have a very positive attitude towards God in general without maintaining any sense of thankfulness toward Him in particular.

Thankfulness requires two critical understandings: *what* and *who*.

- WHAT: We must be conscious of a benefit received. We must realize we are a recipient of something beneficial. We must acknowledge that we have received it.

- WHO: We must be conscious of the giver of the benefit received. We must realize the giver acted knowingly and willingly. We must acknowledge the giver.

Thankfulness requires us to recognize that something of benefit has been received. If something has been received, something has been given; something cannot come from nothing. Who has given it? If something has only been received and not given, the recipient can only feel lucky or fortunate, in the right place at the right time, as the adage goes. A benefactor of chance cannot express thankfulness; whom would she thank? Chance does not have ears to hear, nor a heart to appreciate the return of a thankful word.

Thankfulness requires recognition of a knowing, willing giver. If the benefit received was without the giver's knowledge or will, then he didn't actually give anything. At best the benefit was appropriated or stolen, and once again thankfulness would not be the fitting response.

You are a recipient. Do you realize this? God has knowingly and willingly given to you. What have you received? For what are you thankful? Honestly assess this. Do you struggle to come up with one thing? Or could you fill up pages?

_____

_____

_____

_____

EYE ON THE GIVER

God is a giving God. A quick search in Bible Gateway of "God gives" identifies 33 times in the Old and New Testaments where God gives something of value or benefit. This is certainly not an exhaustive list from scripture but just a

WEEK 4: THANKSGIVING, DAY 2

quick search to get us started thinking about our generous, giving Father.

God gives...

☐ rest ☐ land ☐ victory ☐ power ☐ wealth ☐ safety

☐ rain ☐ songs ☐ strength ☐ honor ☐ spirit ☐ seasons

☐ body ☐ Holy Spirit ☐ growth ☐ wisdom ☐ grace ☐ light

☐ life ☐ possessions ☐ territory ☐ authority ☐ breath

Even as I write, other generous gifts come to my mind:

☐ love ☐ gentleness ☐ joy ☐ self-control

☐ hope ☐ peace ☐ kindness ☐ healing

What about you? What gifts of God would you add?

☐ _____ ☐ _____ ☐ _____

☐ _____ ☐ _____ ☐ _____

☐ _____ ☐ _____ ☐ _____

Are you thankful for any of these personally? Put a checkmark next to any you would thank God for today.

WHAT ELSE DOES GOD GIVE?

Good things that we cannot even imagine to ask for come from our heavenly Father's generous hand. For me, He has given Evelyn Davison, my beautiful mentor and radio co-host who is 90 years old and has been speaking, writing, and doing radio for over 35 years. She refers to thanksgiving in prayer as a time for "pause and applaud." What a fun way to see this special time in prayer! God's Word highlights three particular ways God gives to us. We can pause and applaud our Heavenly Father for His great:

    PROVISION   FAVOR   BLESSING

What does God's PROVISION look like and how do we recognize it?

MY VOICE, HIS HEART

Provision is something prepared and provided—generally food, clothing, or equipment, especially for a journey—by forethought or providential care.

Please underline above "by forethought and providential care." Let's break those apart.

Forethought is careful consideration of what will be necessary or may happen in the future. *Providence* is the protective care of God or timely preparation for future events.[8]

When we think of *provision*, we can recognize God in His protective care for us. We can know that He has carefully considered what will be necessary. We can be fully aware that He has made timely preparation for us in our journey.

What has God *provided* for you this year? Be as specific as you can.

_____

_____

_____

_____

_____

_____

_____

_____

Now, go back and consider each provision you listed. If it was a NEED God provided for, put an N in front of it. If it was a DESIRE or want God provided for, put a D in front of it.

Is your vision beginning to shift and refocus? May we be wide-eyed with

WEEK 4: THANKSGIVING, DAY 2

amazement when we begin to recognize the countless provisions, the undeserved favor, and the blessing upon blessing we have received from the generous hand of God!

Let's close today with a time of thanksgiving in prayer. Tomorrow we will dig deeper into what God's Word teaches us about favor and blessing. I can hardly wait.

"Father, I lift my eyes to You, Who sits enthroned in heaven. You are the generous Giver of life and all good things. You have carefully considered my needs. With Your protective care You have prepared provision for me. You have knowingly and willingly given all I need from Your hand. My days You have numbered, and given purpose to each one. By Your Spirit You pour into my deepest needs. You never forsake me, not ever. When I consider all this, my spirit is filled with thanksgiving. With my voice I thank You.
I thank You specifically for... [*give thanks to Him for everything you check-marked under 'God Gives' as well as all He has provided for you this year*].
These words of thanksgiving I lift to Your throne in Jesus' name. Amen."[9]

DAY 3

Week 4: Thanksgiving

"I thank You, LORD, for Your steadfast love. I thank You for Your wondrous works in my life. You satisfy my longing soul and fill me to overflowing with good things. Your gates open before me as I approach; thanksgiving fills my heart all the more. You run to meet me before a word of praise is formed on my lips. My Father and my God, You are my blessing and my very great reward.
[*Share your own words of thanksgiving as we open together today.*]
In Jesus' name I pray. Amen."[10]

THE FAVOR OF A KING

I love that my friends can always be counted on to help this girl out. I enjoy returning the favor whenever I can. These special favors, and my ability to reciprocate, make me thankful for the friendship community I have.

This is often what we think of when we consider what favor looks like. However, *favor* from God is a whole new realm of favor. It is a special something that will burst our hearts open with thanksgiving when we comprehend it rightly. We are not talking here about any simple favor from a friend. This is not a matter of filling in at carpool, picking up the coffee tab, or help with a task. Let's take a look at what favor from God looks like.

The word *favor* appears over 140 times in God's Word. It is translated from the Hebrew words *chen*, *chanan*, and *paniym* (although far less from this last one) and from the Greek word *charis*.

A more complete translation of favor would include:

- Kindness
- Face
- Front
- Encamp
- Mercy
- Abide
- Incline
- Delight
- Grace

MY VOICE, HIS HEART

- Acceptance
- Benefit given
- To bend or stoop to show consideration
- Charm (I love that Jesus is charming)
- Success
- Health
- Well
- Safe

This takes my breath away. This is the favor God extends to every believer in Christ. Imagine it with me. Let's get a clear vision of our loving Father, the Almighty King, seated on His heavenly throne, surrounded by light, beauty, and perfection. Angels are worshipping, and all creation is held together in Him. He sees us. His heart delights. He bends down, stooping low, inclines His ear, accepts us, gives grace to our feeble words, and responds with kindness and mercy. He even encamps around us if needed.

Why would He extend this type of favor to us? Because He loves us intimately. He is our Father and we are His children. We are His treasured possession.[11] I pray we will come to treasure Him above all else, for where our treasure is, there our hearts will be also.[12]

Take a moment and check each aspect of *favor* you have personally experienced. You might even jot down next to the word a reminder of the circumstances surrounding the favor you received.

Next, go back and circle or highlight any aspect of favor you have not experienced but would like to ask God to show you. We will come back to this next week.

RECOGNIZING FAVOR

What does favor feel and look like? How are we to recognize it? The best way I can describe a sense of God's favor is that it feels like unmerited acceptance and kindness that is holding you up when circumstances should be wearing you down. It is like someone watching your back and bringing you success, whether in a relationship, at work, or in a difficult situation. Sometimes it's achieving something and realizing you would never have been able to attain it on your own. On occasion it is a gentle joy and peace when sadness and worry would seem to make the most sense.

My great-great-grandmother escaped from Vilna, Russia during the pogroms in the late 1800s. Her father, the Chief Rabbi in Vilna, remained to help his people as much as he could. He arranged for his only daughter and young

WEEK 4: THANKSGIVING, DAY 3

son to be smuggled out of the city at night in the underside of a carriage to a ship headed for America.

Three generations later, my mother was studying the Old Testament and saw the repeated mention of the three Persons in the One True God. She read through the New Testament as an historical document and saw how this person, Jesus Christ of Nazareth, fulfilled over 60 prophecies for the promised Messiah—prophecies which were written hundreds of years earlier in the Torah. She read the words of Jesus, who declared himself to be One with God, and who referred to God as his Father. She read how Jesus promised to send His Spirit, God's Spirit, to be present and dwell within his followers.

My mother was torn. Raised in Orthodox Judaism, she was forbidden from even speaking the name Jesus; yet she could not deny that this God, Whom she deeply loved, had kept His promise and sent His Son as a Savior to His people. The Messiah she had hoped for all her life was Jesus Christ. She turned to Jesus as the promised Christ and her personal Savior. She was immediately cast out from the family and disowned.

There is a priestly blessing that every Jew knows. If every Christian knows John 3:16, every Jew knows Numbers 6:24-26. It is the blessing the first High Priest, Aaron, spoke over the people of Israel. This is a coveted blessing among the Jewish people. I have it for you here:

> *"The LORD bless you and keep you;*
> *the LORD make His <u>face</u> to shine upon you*
> *and be <u>gracious</u> to you;*
> *the LORD lift up His <u>countenance upon</u> you*
> *and give you peace."*

You will notice that I underlined some words. These words are the same words that can also be translated as *favor*.

While I would never arbitrarily change words of scripture, and I strongly caution against picking and choosing words that twist scripture to say something different than what is intended, I want for a moment to show you the importance of God's favor to His people.

MY VOICE, HIS HEART

Fill in the following blanks with the word *favor* and read the entire scripture out loud as you do.

> "The LORD bless you and keep you; the LORD make His _____ to shine upon you and be _____[able] to you; the LORD lift up His _____ upon you and give you peace."

The favor of God has been the coveted blessing of His people for millennia. The book of Hebrews in the New Testament establishes Jesus as our personal High Priest. Are you ready for this? Prepare yourself...

The favor of God is our personal blessing through Jesus Christ, our High Priest. Therefore, we can also read the priestly blessing like this—write in your name on the blanks and read the entire scripture out loud as you do.

> "Through Christ Jesus, the LORD blesses _____ and keeps _____; the LORD makes His face to shine upon _____ and is gracious to _____; the LORD lifts up His countenance upon _____ and gives _____ peace."

AMEN! THANK YOU, FATHER!

What evidence of God's personal FAVOR can you see in your life?

_____

_____

_____

_____

_____

_____

WEEK 4: THANKSGIVING, DAY 3

Now, back to my mom. (You didn't honestly think I would leave you with "cast out and disowned," did you?) This is what I want to tell you: My mother's family of dedicated, Orthodox Jews saw God's favor so evident in my mother's life over the following few years, that they also came to know Jesus Christ as the Son of God and the Promised Messiah.

I want to clarify here that what they saw was not worldly success, but the priestly blessing resting on her life. God provided for her needs when everything was stacked against her. Rather than being sad and anxious or rebellious and rude, she had a gentle joy and peace. God's favor toward one child was a winsome light that led a family to salvation.

My heart bursts with thanksgiving to God for His favor because it meant I got to grow up in a home with a great-grandmother who loved the name of Jesus Christ. One of my best childhood memories is falling asleep at night listening to the prayers she lifted up to God from her bed—prayers made for each of us by name, filled with thanksgiving for God's goodness, His provision, His favor, and His many blessings.

Tomorrow we will talk about blessings. I am just as giddy about what God is going to show us tomorrow as I was yesterday about today. Is your vision getting lighter and brighter? That often happens when we see God more clearly and thankfulness fills our heart and overflows into our entire spirit.

As my hands move across this keyboard to accomplish the work He has set before me, I can feel His favor.

It is my greatest desire for you that as He moves mightily across your whole life—in your heart, mind, spirit, body, past, present, and future—you also will sense His favor and give Him thanks all the more.

As we close in prayer today, I will leave you with one more beautiful verse in scripture that is a prayer of mine.

> "Let the favor of the Lord our God be upon us,
> and establish the work of our hands for us;
> yes, establish the work of our hands!" Psalm 90:17

MY VOICE, HIS HEART

CLOSING PRAYER

"Thank You, Father God! Thank You a thousand times for Your countless provisions and favor that I have not rightly seen or acknowledged. I thank You now for them. Thank You for opening my eyes to Your provision. Thank You for opening my heart to see Your favor. You have loved me with an everlasting love and have been patient and kind as I have fumbled and stumbled about. Thank You for bending down and inclining Your ear to hear me. Thank You for encamping around me.

[*Give voice to your own words of thanksgiving for the favor God has shown you.*]

I love You and I love how You care for me. In the saving name of Jesus, the Name above all names, I pray. Amen."[13]

WEEK 4: THANKSGIVING, DAY

DAY 4

Week 4: Thanksgiving

"Thank You, Father, for Your inexhaustible love. Thank You for Your breath in my lungs and Your Spirit in my heart. Thank You for the moon and stars that declare Your glory as I sleep. Thank You for this day You have made! Thank You for the rain You send on both the righteous and unrighteous. Thank You for the rising sun that obeys Your command each day to bring light and dispatch the darkness. Thank You for teaching me Your ways that I might walk in them. In Jesus' name, amen."[14]

THANKSGIVING FOR PROVISION, FAVOR AND BLESSING

Oh, my friend, we have so much to give God thanks for. In order to understand *blessing*, we first needed to understand provision and favor. I hope we have accomplished that.

So how is God's blessing different from His provision and favor?

- PROVISION is *enough*. It is a met need, when and where it is needed. We can be satisfied and content with God's provision for us.

- FAVOR is *unmerited benefit or success*; generally, in something in which we have somehow put forth some degree of effort, even if very little.

- BLESSING is favor and provision combined, with a little extra something special added. It is MORE than enough, given by God's hand because of Who He is and not because of what we have earned.

What are you most thankful for today?

☐ PROVISION   ☐ FAVOR   ☐ BLESSING

In an effort to clarify and differentiate between these three, let us keep our eye on the Giver, and consider the best He has given.

Provision is having a Savior who has paid the penalty of death for our sins, affording us eternal life. *Favor* is the Holy Spirit dwelling within us, giving us power over sin and fellowship with God. *Blessing* is being able to enjoy an intimate relationship with God, knowing Him as our Father and receiving His care as His children.

Do you see? God could have stopped at provision and we could have been perfectly content—after all, who can't be content with eternal life? He could have stopped at favor and we would have been filled to abundance—power and fellowship, how amazing is that. Yet He did not stop at provision or favor but proceeded to blessing us all the more with the mind-blowing addition of an intimate relationship with Him. We get to call the Creator of the Universe *Abba, Daddy, Father*.[15] Life cannot get any better than that.

Friend, let us never allow our thanksgiving to be limited to the provisions of God. Let us pour out thanksgiving for His great favor and many blessings.

Let's take some time to recognize all we have received from God. Obviously, we could fill hundreds of pages on this. Today, we will focus on what has been most meaningful, impactful, or life-changing for us. Put a star next to anything you would be willing to share with others. If you are having a hard time getting started, go back to Days 2 and 3 of this week and use some provisions and favors we have already identified.

PROVISION	FAVOR	BLESSING

WEEK 4: THANKSGIVING, DAY 4

BLESSINGS MULTIPLIED

The Bible is filled with blessings given by God. The first time we see the word *blessing* is in the first book of the Bible, Genesis, in chapter 12, where God laid out an incredible principle attached to blessing. It is this:

We will receive blessing from God
and so shall we be a blessing to others.

This applies to you, me, and every follower of Christ. We are to receive the blessings of God, and we are to be a blessing to others. God has built in a multiplier effect when we do not hold tightly to the blessings we are given but are generous in giving blessings to others.[16]

Jesus tells us: "Freely you have received; freely give."[17] The Apostle Paul recalls Jesus emphasizing, "It is more blessed to give than receive."[18] God gives us an extra blessing as we give to others. Jesus says we will receive additional blessings from God "poured into our lap" with the same measure that we use to give to others, but God's measure will be "pressed down, shaken together, and running over."[19]

Are you seeing that God loves to bless, and He loves to see His children bless others? When we are thankful for all God has given and know He desires to give even more, we tend <u>not</u> to hold onto what we have so tightly. That is a blessing in itself. Go back and quickly highlight in the above paragraph the verse that speaks to you the most about this principle of receiving and giving blessing.

There is another special aspect to blessing:

Blessing is given not only for the present but also
as a promise or assurance for the future.

In Genesis 15:5 and 18:18, God blesses Abraham with the blessing that he would become a great nation and his offspring would be so numerous that they could not be counted. We see Isaac's blessing for Jacob in Genesis 27:27-29. Jacob as well gives a blessing to each of his sons for their present and future in Genesis 49. If you are interested, you can take a look at these scriptures for yourself now, or save that for another time.

Today, we can be thankful not only for the blessings of the past but also for the blessings of the future.

At a women's retreat I attended in my 30s, one of the speakers highlighted Revelation 1:8. This scripture tells us that God is the Almighty who was and is and is to come. We need to realize that He is God over our *was*, our *is*, and our *is to come*. Some of us have a pretty messed up *was*. Only God can bless our *was* by redeeming it. Only He can bless our *is* by meeting our deepest need. Only He can bless and secure each day of our *is to come*.

During times of thanksgiving in prayer, we typically look back, reflect, and remember those things for which we are thankful. We need to know that thanksgiving is not meant to only recognize benefits of the past, but also to acknowledge we have received future blessings in our present. In Hebrews chapter 11, God commends people throughout history who were looking forward to something they had not yet received, something that had only been promised to them. God says they saw these promises from a distance and "greeted them" or "received them joyfully."[20] When God promises something for our *is to come*, we can be thankful for the blessing now because we know He holds our future secure.

Are there any blessings you are thankful for today that God has promised for your future?

_____

_____

_____

_____

_____

As you close out your time with God in prayer today, spend time in thanksgiving for the many blessings He has poured out over your life, as well the promises He has given you for your *is to come*.

WEEK 4: THANKSGIVING, DAY 4

I hope you are becoming more comfortable with voicing your prayers. I continue to feel the excitement build in me knowing that, as you grow in prayer, He is going to open doors and hearts to you that you never imagined you would approach. You are doing great! Big hugs to you, my friend.

"Father, You are the Almighty Who was and is and is to come. Thank You that my past, present and future are secure in You alone. Thank You for Your countless blessings over my life.

Today I give you specific thanks for [*give voice to your own words of thanksgiving for His many blessings over your past, present and future*].

I pray in the name of my Lord and Savior, Jesus Christ, my greatest blessing of all. Amen."[21]

WEEK 4: THANKSGIVING, DAY

DAY 5

Week 4: Thanksgiving

OPENING PRAYER

"Gracious Father, You comfort me and look with compassion on all my hurts and heartache. You promise that You will make the dry places in my soul like Eden. You will make my wastelands like the Garden of the LORD and we will walk together. Joy and gladness overflow from my heart for these blessings. You alone, God, will accomplish this. Let thanksgiving and the sound of singing be heard from my lips all my days. I give my life to You. I align my will to Yours. With thanksgiving overflowing from my cup I pray. Amen."[22]

THE SACRIFICE OF THANKSGIVING

I am not ready for this to be the last day of our week of thanksgiving. We have something to discuss that is so beautiful and important. I desperately want to do it justice and communicate well. Stick with me as we are going to take a few turns today from the very simple to something I believe is a mystery revealed.

By now we have our eyes open to the truth that there is so much for which we can be thankful. If thankfulness is being conscious of the benefit received and thankfulness acknowledges the Giver, why is thankfulness not enough? Why must we press into thanksgiving?

God's word says, "In everything *give thanks*."[23]

In the Old Testament there was a special, voluntary offering referred to as the "sacrifice of thanksgiving." This offering was to be presented with a heart of joy and gratitude, with hands extended into the air. As it was considered a peace offering, portions were shared between God, the priest, and the worshipper. This communion of sorts emphasized one's relationship with and nearness to God. Unlike other peace offerings, the sacrifice of thanksgiving was unique in that the worshipper's portion would then be shared with one's family and friends, expanding the sense of generosity and communion. Thanksgiving is a sacrifice that brings us closer to God as well as to those around us.

There is another historical account in the Bible that I love. Turn to Luke 17 in your Bible and read verses 11-19. This event occurred when Jesus was passing between the regions of Samaria and Galilee on his way to Jerusalem.

1. Who met Jesus?

☐ His disciples ☐ Lepers ☐ Pharisees ☐ Shepherds

2. How many were there?

☐ 3 ☐ 5 ☐ 10 ☐ 100s

3. What did they ask Jesus for?

☐ Mercy ☐ An explanation ☐ Teaching ☐ Prayer

4. How did Jesus respond?

☐ With Scripture ☐ A Parable ☐ Food ☐ Healing

5. How many returned to see Jesus again?

☐ All ☐ 1 ☐ Half ☐ 2

6. What was the purpose of returning to see Jesus?

☐ Questions ☐ Rebuke ☐ Thanksgiving ☐ Prayer

7. What was Jesus' response?

☐ He gave the great Sermon on the Mount.
☐ He spoke firmly to them for not believing and encouraged them to do better.
☐ He was amazed that only 1 returned to give thanks when all had received their request.
☐ He wept and prayed for them.

Jesus uses the life of this lowly Samaritan leper to clearly establish the right response to receiving: giving thanks, without delay. Scripture says, "In everything give thanks;" we might add, "right away."

WEEK 4: THANKSGIVING, DAY 5

We are prone to question "in everything." Surely, not everything that happens to us is worth thanking God for. There is no question that many evil and difficult things happen, events filled with turmoil, sorrow, and tragedy. However, what the scriptures address is our response amidst these events. If at the moment we are unable to give thanks *for* everything, that is okay. Let's be gentle with ourselves and trust God that in accordance with His promise to us, He will ultimately use even these unwanted circumstances for our good and His glory.[24]

We can see examples of this principle by returning to where we started on Day 1. Remember David fleeing for his life and Paul in jail? God used these men and all of their experiences to build the character of a mighty King in whose line Jesus would come as Savior of the world, and to establish His church that all nations would know the love of God, forgiveness of sins, and the truth of eternal life. Yes friend, God will never allow anything into our lives that He cannot use for our good. In everything we truly can give thanks.

I, with tongue in cheek, refer to the healed leper as an example in scripture of a "First Responder." In America we are struggling with an historic lack of thankfulness and thanksgiving. We live in thankless times. Children no longer thank their parents for providing shelter, food, and clothing. Parents no longer thank employers for providing a job. Church members often fail to thank those that serve them. A growing number of Americans are no longer thankful for this amazing nation in which God has blessed us to live.

We are seeing this creep into God's church. We have twisted God's gracious provision, favor, and blessing into entitlement guarantees. Even preachers have begun to tell members what they want to hear: that all that God has for them is health, wealth, and prosperity. They are selling the lie that anything less would be beneath our status as children of a King. This distorts both God's goodness and man's need.

God is perfect, holy, and righteous. God owes us nothing. We are sinful, wayward, and warped. We owe Him everything. If we do not start from this place of truth and proper humility, our basis for giving thanks will be selfishly entitled and limited. We must not allow our hearts to be overcome with the darkness of thanklessness. We do not have to be in a good mood in order to give God thanks; but it is amazing how giving thanks will change our mood and result in a lifted spirit.

When we are pressed and hurting, we can still give thanks to the LORD, for He is good and His steadfast love endures forever.[25] Thanksgiving is anchored in the steadfast, eternal love of God. Let's keep our eyes on Him and aspire to be a First Responder.

We give thanks for each breath today; we have no guarantee there will be life in our lungs tomorrow. We give thanks for shelter, every meal, and the simple rhythms of life. We can give thanks for the person honking his horn because it means we can hear. We can give thanks for the 6:30 a.m. alarm because it means we have a job. We can give thanks for the sink full of dirty dishes because it means we have food to eat.

In your life have you tended to be like the nine lepers who walked away, or have you tended to be the one who does an about-face and responds immediately with thanksgiving?

What can you give thanks for today that you had not considered giving thanks for previously?

_____

_____

_____

_____

THE ULTIMATE THANKSGIVING

Are you familiar with church communion, also called the holy sacrament, eucharist, or Lord's Supper? I have to share something I recently learned about communion that deepened my commitment to thanksgiving.

The cup of wine, or juice, which symbolizes the blood of Christ, first symbolized the blood of the Passover lamb which saved the Hebrew people from the curse of death.[26] This cup is referred to by the Jewish people as the Cup of Thanksgiving.[27] The last supper Christ ate with his disciples before going to the cross was the Passover meal. Jesus, as he picked up the Cup of Thanksgiving, proclaimed, "This is a new covenant in my blood which is poured out for you."[28]

WEEK 4: THANKSGIVING, DAY 5

Every time we participate in communion, we are literally lifting up the Cup of Thanksgiving as we remember the blood of Jesus Christ as the sacrificial atonement for our sins which saved us from the curse of death.[29] It is as if God is saying, "I gave my Son so your cup could overflow with thanksgiving." Thanksgiving is a beautiful spring that overflows from a thankful heart. Let us remember that thankfulness cannot be seen or heard unless it is expressed in thanksgiving. Our thanksgiving may be the light that leads others to Christ. Thanksgiving is the humble expression of our thankfulness and can satisfy the soul and energize the spirit like little else. On Love Talk Radio, we have a saying: Thanksgiving is the key to Thanks-living.

CLOSING PRAYER

"Thankfulness overflows from my heart, LORD, for You are good and Your love endures forever. Receive my words of thanksgiving as I enter Your gates and proceed into Your magnificent courts.
[*Enjoy ending this week thanking Him for all He has taught You. This is only the beginning, friend; He has so much more for you. Close the prayer in your own words. I will simply add my agreement with an amen.*]
Amen."[30]

"My fellow believers, whether we like it or not, asking is the rule of the kingdom."
CHARLES SPURGEON

"I cried unto the LORD with my voice; with my voice did I make supplication."
PSALM 142:1 (KJV)

Week Five

WEEK 5: SUPPLICATION, DAY

DAY 1

Week 5: Supplication

OPENING PRAYER

"Gracious LORD, You alone are God. There is no other like You. You alone redeem, restore, and refresh Your children, for Your name's sake. Your judgement is right and Your decisions are blameless. My mouth declares Your praise. My sin is against You alone. Be gracious to me, according to Your lovingkindness. I come humbly before You and ask You to forgive me. Wash me thoroughly from my sin. Remove my transgressions from before my face, blot them out and cast them away. Create in me a clean heart and renew a steadfast spirit within me. Open my ears to Your voice, my eyes to Your glory, and my heart to Your joy. I love You, my God and Father. In Jesus' holy name I pray. Amen."[1]

SUPPLI-WHAT?

I've been looking forward to this week together, possibly more than any other week. Supplication is the asking part of prayer. I am mentally rubbing my hands together like an excited schoolgirl. How about you?

Supplication comes from the Greek word *deesis*, meaning to earnestly or humbly ask from a place of need or indigence. Asking comes naturally to us. We don't generally have to think hard or figure out our words when there is something we need or want. We simply open our mouth and our requests, wants, and desires pop right out.

With grunts and cries an infant makes requests known; toddlers point; a young child looks up with longing eyes, a simple "pweasc" is enough when vocabulary is still developing. Our teenagers do not need to form a robust, persuasive request each night in order to be given dinner. We know they are hungry, we know what their growing bodies need, and we are happy to supply healthy food for them in the right amount and at the right time.

God not only is generous in how He meets our physical needs,[2] but He addresses our deeper emotional and spiritual needs with a firm promise.

MY VOICE, HIS HEART

When we think of prayer, approaching God with our many asks is largely what comes to mind, and rightly it should. God wants us to come with our requests. He encourages and even commands that we do. When my husband and I sent our oldest off to college we gave her strict instructions that she was to call us immediately if there was anything she needed. We told her she was not to hesitate for a second. God tells us the same.

A PROMISE GIVEN

God gives us clear instruction in prayer as well as a unique promise:

> "Do not be anxious about anything, but in everything by prayer and supplication with thanksgiving let your requests be made known to God. And the peace of God, which surpasses all understanding, will guard your hearts and minds in Christ Jesus." Philippians 4:6-7

1. What does God say we should be anxious about?

☐ Salvation   ☐ Finances   ☐ Children

☐ Health   ☐ Everything   ☐ Nothing

2. In regard to what, does God say we should go to Him with our requests?

☐ Salvation   ☐ Finances   ☐ Children

☐ Health   ☐ Everything   ☐ Nothing

3. What extra does God promise to give even though we didn't ask for it?

☐ Nothing   ☐ Prosperity   ☐ Peace

☐ Understanding ☐ A Quick Answer

4. What are the attributes of God's peace highlighted here?

☐ His peace guards our hearts   ☐ His peace guards our minds

☐ His peace surpasses all understanding   ☐ All the above

WEEK 5: SUPPLICATION, DAY 1

I have to tell you, this scripture transformed my prayer life when I wrapped my head and heart around what God is communicating to us here. I bought a ridiculously large 6' x 8' wall hanging with this scripture printed on it and hung it in my entry way as a reminder that in all my comings and goings, in everything, I could live in a place of peace—mind-blowing peace that surpasses the understanding of even the greatest spiritual thinkers. Peace that is promised and given straight from the throne of God. And all it requires is one simple activity: prayer. Prayer that asks. Prayer that makes requests known to God—not because He needs informing, but because He desires us to exchange concern about our needs for confidence in His provision.

A STEADFAST ASSURANCE

So much scripture is written commanding and encouraging us to ask, seek, knock, request, and petition God in prayer. Scripture assures us God will answer, provide, open doors, and give good things. I have been warned (possibly you have, too) to make sure I never take advantage of God or abuse Him by regarding Him as a vending-machine or a magical genie of sorts. These cautions tend to make me giggle a little because they assume something ridiculous: that we are somehow able to take advantage of God or abuse Him.

While we are horribly off base if we deign to treat God as a genie, let me assure you, friend, we cannot possibly take advantage of God enough. Drawing near to God in prayer with our needs and requests is never abuse; it is beautiful and desired by Him. If our view of God is as small as that of a magical genie, we are not taking advantage of Him, but we are instead limiting our expectations. God is infinitely more powerful than any genie we can imagine, and we get more than three requests. Likewise, if we view God as a vending machine, we are getting short-changed, because unlike a vending machine, God's possibilities and resources are limitless.

We certainly must approach the throne of God with awe and reverence. Nothing else is fitting. If our understanding of God does not evoke this in us, we are not seeing God rightly. No matter how arrogant, confident, or superior we are in our own eyes, when we come before the God of the universe, the Creator of all things seen and unseen,[3] we can have no other response but all-surpassing wonder. Let's ask big, expectantly, and extravagantly. May nothing keep us from going to God with our requests.

MY VOICE, HIS HEART

I want you to look up some scriptures and write them out. While you are writing, keep three fundamentals keenly before you:

- The *character* of the God you are asking. He is eternally loving, fully righteous, and extravagantly generous.
- The *power* of the God you are asking. He is omnipotent, omniscient, omnipresent, Almighty God.
- The *resources* of the God you are asking. He is the infinite Creator of all.

Please highlight in your Bible and record the following scriptures below.

Psalm 107:6

_____

_____

Jeremiah 33:3

_____

_____

Matthew 21:22

_____

_____

Luke 11:9-10

_____

_____

WEEK 5: SUPPLICATION, DAY 1

John 14:14

_____

_____

John 15:7

_____

_____

Philippians 4:19

_____

_____

James 1:5

_____

_____

I know that was a lot of work and took more time than we usually do, but I hope each verse sparked an eagerness in you to pray more enthusiastically with your requests. Supplication in prayer is not limited to our basic needs. Supplication extends to our desires, wants, longings, and aspirations. Nothing is beyond asking in prayer, and God will supply beyond what we can ask or imagine.[4]

I love the way my friend Sylvia sums up the principles of supplication in her "Prayer for Beginners" MP3 download. If you are incorporating it with this study, she will wrap up our time together today and give you some insights into what is ahead this week. If not, let's take a deep breath and prepare to close together in prayer. We've learned a lot today. Thank you for pressing deeper into relationship with me. I imagine your beautiful face as I write this and I thank God for you. You are God's answer to my requests and desires.

MY VOICE, HIS HEART

INTERACTIVE PRAYER DOWNLOAD

If you are using the Let's Pray Today Ministries "Prayer for Beginners" mp3 download, go to the Prayer #4 on track 5. Listen and pray all the way through to the end of Prayer #4 (approx. 7 minutes). You may use the prayer as your closing prayer for today, or join in the one below.

"Generous, loving Father, I thank You for Your open ear and generous hand. I long to share every desire of my heart with you. Purify my heart, LORD, and forgive me for unholy desires I have held onto in either willful disobedience or ignorance. I do not want any desire in me that is undesirable to You. I thank You for the desires of my heart that You have given me. You know my longings, my dreams, and my needs. I bring them to Your throne and ask for Your provision, favor, and blessing.

[*Bring any needs, requests, or desires to God that are on your heart.*]

Thank You, Father. I love You. In the mighty name of Your Son, I pray. Amen."[5]

WEEK 5: SUPPLICATION, DAY

DAY 2

Week 5: Supplication

OPENING PRAYER

Would you please pen and voice a prayer to open us today?

"_____

_____

_____

_____

_____

_____. Amen."

THE OBVIOUS TRUTH

My three teenage daughters tend to roll their eyes when I point out something they deem as obvious. When I was a teenager, we would accompany the eye roll with a silent *Duh*. At the risk of causing you a spiritual eye roll, or worse, I am going to highlight something that may already be apparent to you but is very important nonetheless: we did not open this prayer study with supplication. Actually, we have not begun prayer once with a request, but instead with adoration, confession, and thanksgiving.

There is good reason for this. Throughout scripture God highlights eleven reasons He will either refuse to listen to our prayers or simply not answer them. By spending time with Him in adoration and confession, we purposefully draw close to Him and are in a position for Him to work in our heart and mind, opening our eyes to anything that is breaking our relationship with Him and allowing us to respond by acknowledging the sin, turning from it, and in some cases setting it right. I am not going to spend time on these eleven matters today but I have covered them in the Appendix (see #11 of the True & False Review we completed in Week 1).

MY VOICE, HIS HEART

By spending additional time in thanksgiving before engaging in supplication, we are enabled to see the provision, favor, and blessing we have already received. This confirms in our spirit to Whom we belong and how beautifully He cares for us. It also tends to calm our heart and make us less frantic about the immediate needs before us.

We might begin to think that the more we grow in relationship with God and the more we spend time in spiritual mindfulness and awareness of His glory throughout our day, the less important adoration, confession, and thanksgiving in prayer become because we are abiding in Him and walking in His ways. We might reason that we have achieved a level of closeness and maturity and can therefore ask away unhindered as the focus of prayer. There is an element of truth in this.

However, the more we draw near to God in worship, study, and prayer, the more fully we will understand and experience His love and goodness, and the more we will desire to draw near to Him in prayer with adoration, confession, and thanksgiving. If we find ourselves only coming to God in prayer because we are pressed by need, desperate in circumstances, or heartbroken by loss, we have wandered from His side.

Friend, we can be eternally thankful for the grace of God that uses our needs, circumstances, and heartbreaks to draw us to Him in prayer. Let us, however, guard our hearts from becoming so puffed up that we abandon adoration, confession, and thanksgiving.

Now, let's dive in and ask big, expect much, and request even more.

ASKING BIG

On Week 4, Day 2, in the section "God Gives," we highlighted some benefits in scripture that God specifically gives. In the exercise, you marked any items for which you were thankful. Take a second look at the benefits below and mark any items you desire today in your life.

Our God loves to give generously. We are going to ask Him for these desires we have.

- ☐ rest
- ☐ land
- ☐ victory
- ☐ power
- ☐ wealth

- ☐ rain
- ☐ songs
- ☐ strength
- ☐ honor
- ☐ safety

WEEK 5: SUPPLICATION, DAY 2

- ☐ spirit
- ☐ wisdom
- ☐ territory
- ☐ kindness
- ☐ self-control
- ☐ seasons
- ☐ grace
- ☐ breath
- ☐ hope
- ☐ body
- ☐ light
- ☐ peace
- ☐ healing
- ☐ Holy Spirit
- ☐ possessions
- ☐ authority
- ☐ gentleness
- ☐ growth
- ☐ life
- ☐ love
- ☐ joy

What would you add that you would like to request from God? Be as specific as you can.

_____

_____

_____

_____

Look up a scripture that assures you God gives one or more of the specific items you marked or wrote out. You can use the concordance at the back of your bible to find a scripture or a bible search site or app (my favorite is biblegateway.com).

Scripture dealing with: _____ _____

Scripture Reference (Book, chapter:verse) _____

_____

_____

_____

_____.

151

MY VOICE, HIS HEART

Today we will close in prayer by enjoying the liberty we have in confidently asking big things from our great God. If you had difficulty finding a scripture today, go back and select one of the scriptures you looked up yesterday that struck a chord in your heart. Voice the desires you marked today as well as the request you wrote out, referencing your selected scripture in prayer. We are going to learn more about praying scripture tomorrow.

CLOSING PRAYER

"Father, Thank You for Your Word to me. It is a lamp to my feet and a light to my path. You tell me in Your Word that You delight in me and that when I draw near to You, You draw near to me. You tell me to bring You my desires and go to You with all my needs.

I know I am not worthy of such esteem and it is with Your grace and love that You lavish such honor on me. I believe and trust the truth of Your Word to me and bring my desires and requests before Your throne.

[*Share with God everything you have marked and written on the previous page, as well as the assurance you have in scripture that establishes this is given by God.*]

How I desire and need Your goodness and love, LORD. I longed for it before I knew it was mine for the asking. My spirit bows to the presence of Your Spirit—the same Spirit that raised my Savior Jesus from death to life. In His name I pray. Amen."[6]

WEEK 5: SUPPLICATION, DAY

DAY 3

Week 5: Supplication

"Have mercy on me, O God, according to Your steadfast love. A broken and contrite heart, God, You will not despise. Strengthen my legs to stand in the times You have chosen for me. Create in me a clean heart, O God; and renew a steadfast spirit in me. I desire to be filled with Your love, Your truth, and Your wisdom. Bring me into the joy of Your salvation and grant me a willing spirit to sustain me. Help me to trust amidst trouble, be patient in love, and live humbly in victory. Your love for me is better than life. Open my lips, LORD, and my mouth will declare Your praise. I will proclaim You, my God and Savior, to those who have yet to know You. My heart is for Your holding, my life is for Your glory. I praise You in Jesus' name. Amen."[7]

ASKING WITH HIS WORD

Most of today's opening prayer is from Psalm 51. This is a special Psalm to me because it was penned by King David after he royally messed up and was disciplined by God. David did not rebel in the hard places in life but pressed into relationship with God all the more. No wonder God referred to him as "a man after His [God's] own heart."[8] When difficulty comes, we can know God will not abandon us but will press in all the more as well. We must do the same.

While God gave high commendations to men and women throughout the Bible, one of the highest compliments we might give someone in an everyday context is that of being "a man of his word." Jesus himself holds this up as righteous and honorable.[9]

Friend, this is something I aspire to be: a woman of my word. A woman who does what she says she will do, never a hypocrite, without double-standards, reliable, honest, and truthful. The words I speak and write, I want to be apparent in my life to the extent that others can read without reading and hear without hearing. Oh, that they would be able to examine my comings

MY VOICE, HIS HEART

and goings, my engagements and interactions, my actions and reactions, and be able to hear God's love and read His love letter to them without opening a book or attending an event.

Yet how I fail. Repeatedly. I am astonished at my inability to live up to what I know to be right, true, pleasing, excellent, lovely, and praiseworthy.[10] I'm sure I would be a walking saint if I didn't have children, weren't married, enjoyed perfect health, and lived at a retreat center surrounded in perpetual peaceful bliss; but alas, God has placed all of us in a fallen world with pressures, temptations, and frustrations of every kind. I am grateful for Paul who confesses his failings[11] and encourages us to keep pressing to be women of our word, as we live out His Word.[12]

There is One Person who very literally is "a Man of His Word." The Bible highlights this amazing mystery: "The Word became flesh and made his dwelling among us. We have seen his glory, the glory of the one and only Son, who came from the Father, full of grace and truth."[13] Jesus did not fail to fulfill God's Word, keep God's Word, or manifest God's Word, even for one second. As He walked the earth, He was the love of God on display for men to read without reading. Multitudes heard the love of God rising in their spirits, without words to encumber the joy that overflowed in them.

Grab your highlighter and refer back to the scriptures you looked up and wrote down during our time together in Day 1 of this week. Find the scripture that ties together our prayers, Jesus Christ, and His Word and put a star next to it. Then restate the scripture here using your own words:

_____

_____

_____

_____

The scripture I starred was John 15:7. I love knowing that the words of Jesus can abide in me. If His words abide in me, they become part of me, my thoughts, my will, my life. I can ask whatever I wish in those same abiding words, and He, the very living Word of God, will fulfill those words in

WEEK 5: SUPPLICATION, DAY 3

my asking. What an exquisite mystery. Praying scripture is powerful and intensely personal—our needs and longings are wrapped in God's Word and fulfilled by Christ through the power of the Holy Spirit. Wow. That's what I call asking big.

STEPPING OUT WITH PRAYER AND FAITH

When I first began Let's Pray Today Ministries and completed all the studio work with our authors to record our prayer CDs, I took every little step by prayer and faith. Every prayer we recorded was based on and filled with scripture. We were on a tight budget, our authors were unknown, and none of us had ever worked in a recording studio before. When Kay Arthur, my all-time favorite Bible teacher, endorsed our entire series of prayer CDs, I was overwhelmed with the favor God had shown us.

Standing in line with my daughters waiting to get on The Great White Rollercoaster at Sea World in San Antonio, Texas (best roller coaster ever, by the way), my phone rang and I almost denied the call but answered quickly instead. When the voice on the other end introduced herself as Kay Arthur's assistant from Precept Ministries, I laughed a little, thinking one of my girlfriends was playing a practical joke.

All of a sudden, we were at the front of the line and I was speechless, realizing this was no joke. The ride attendants insisted I get off the phone and onto the rollercoaster. I somehow managed to pull my wits together, mumble out a few words that I hoped communicated I would call her back in 15 minutes, and joined my girls in the front seats of the Great White, screaming our heads off in sheer thrill and joy for the next 120 seconds. I walked on air for the next week at least. As we step out with prayer and faith, we never know where or when God will answer, but we can always know it will be in keeping with His Word.

Kay gave us a wonderful endorsement. Her one suggestion and request for future prayer CDs and materials was that we incorporate even more scripture into our prayers. I have endeavored to honor that request in everything I do in ministry, on radio, and in my life personally. Kay knew then what I have learned since: faith and prayer rooted firmly in God's Word will enable us to step out into broad, open places we never envisioned for ourselves.

HIS WORD, HIS WILL, OUR CONFIDENCE

God's Word abides in God's will. The two are never to be separated. There is great power in God's Word, so much so that when we pull God's Word out of His will, we can do great damage to ourselves and others. Satan knows God's Word but twists it to his own will, using what is meant for life and righteousness to bring death and destruction.[14]

On Day 5 of Week 1, we studied the importance of aligning our will to God's will, and on Week 2, Day 5 we learned how important it is to submit our prayers to God's will. Both of these are achieved as we press into scripture to bring our requests to God in prayer.

If our requests go against scripture, we can know our will is out of alignment with God's will. In that case we need to step back and reconsider where our heart is and why we desire what we request. If our requests align with scripture, we can bring God's own words to His throne, confident all the more that what we are requesting places us securely in unity with the Father, Son, and Spirit. As we abide in this unity in prayer, we essentially become an answer to Jesus' prayer for that same unity in relationship.[15] How breathtaking is that, friend!

No wonder the Apostle John encourages us by writing, "This is the confidence we have in approaching God: that if we ask anything according to His will, He hears us. And if we know that He hears us—whatever we ask—we know that we have what we asked of Him."[16]

HIS WORD, HIS SPIRIT, OUR VICTORY SWORD

Like the legendary King Arthur who pulled the sword out of the rock, we also can reach into our Bible and draw out a mighty sword. Scripture tells us that the Word of God is the Sword of the Spirit.[17] His Word is alive and powerful, sharper than the sharpest two-edged sword.[18] The Word of God applied in unity with the Spirit of God is our victory Sword in this spiritual battle. Let us always remember that "our struggle is not against flesh and blood, but against the rulers, against the authorities, against the powers of this dark world and against the spiritual forces of evil in the heavenly realms."[19] We battle against lies, fear, anxiety, and a host of other dark forces in prayer. May we reach into our Bible and pull out that mighty sword every time.

WEEK 5: SUPPLICATION, DAY 3

SPIRIT + WORD = OUR SWORD

Would you please close us in prayer today? Use one scripture that God has pressed on your heart and include it in your prayer. Take joy to include all your requests! Don't leave one out. Turn back to Day 3 of Week 4, "Favor of a King," and look over every favor you marked that you would like God to show you. Include these in your prayer.

Write out your payer, then go back and give your voice to it as well. God loves the sound of your beautiful voice. He set your vocal cords in place to their exact length and tuned them uniquely to fit who He created you to be. Like me, you may not be able to carry a tune, but you can carry a symphony to heaven in prayer.

CLOSING PRAYER

"_____

_____

_____

_____

_____

_____

_____

_____. Amen."

WEEK 5: SUPPLICATION, DAY

DAY 4

Week 5: Supplication

OPENING PRAYER

"You, O God, are my sun and shield. I wrap myself in the warmth and assurance of Your love for me. You are my confidence and my hope all day long. You give me breath to rise and strength to stand. Forgive my weary thoughts and my complacent effort. Refresh and revive my heart. Invigorate my determination that I would persevere and be faithful in full exertion of life and spirit. Turn my eyes to my neighbor. Fill my heart with Your compassion and love for them. Thank You, LORD of my salvation. In the mighty name of Jesus I pray. Amen."[20]

ASKING BIG FOR ANOTHER

Hannah walked into her evening Bible study group teary-eyed. Her dad had turned himself in that afternoon to begin serving a one-year prison sentence. No one noticed her coming in. They were too busy with each other. All except Faith, a newcomer to the group. Faith gave Hannah a smile and a sweet hello. Quickly, tears began to roll as Hannah shared her heartache and fears with her new friend.

Though Faith didn't know what to say to Hannah, she hugged her and prayed. Faith prayed the one thing she knew for sure—our loving God had a plan for Hannah, her family, and her dad, a plan to help them and not to harm them.[21]

Faith and Hannah captured people's attention as the two of them stood in the room—holding hands, heads down, praying together. Group leaders stood nearby and listened, amazed because Faith and Hannah were only five years old.

The above is a true story. It was tearfully relayed to me via phone by my youngest daughter's AWANA Cubbies leader, who spent several minutes praising Faith's compassion and spiritual maturity.

MY VOICE, HIS HEART

I had to laugh, because while God had given Faith a compassionate heart, she was just like any little girl her age. She wanted to make friends, play with dolls, and be silly. She simply had been raised in a praying family with a praying church. She knew one simple truth: our life, our troubles, and our joys are important to God.

Praying with and for others does not require great spiritual maturity. Let's not miss out on being a blessing because we think we are not ready, not up to it, or not mature enough. As we ask big for ourselves, let's also ask big for others.

Does the idea of praying for someone else make you nervous?

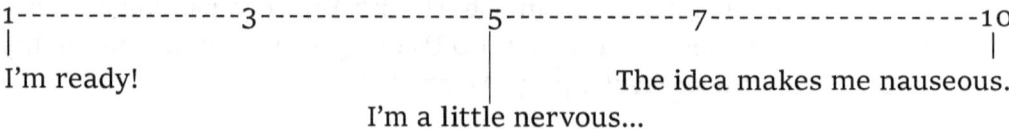

1----------------3-----------------5------------7------------------10
| | |
I'm ready!   The idea makes me nauseous.
                          I'm a little nervous...

If you responded with a 1-3, I encourage you to call a friend, family member, or someone in your Bible study group who's walking through difficult waters. Explain that you are learning to pray for others and would like to pray for them. Ask if you can pray for them at that moment. Trust me when I tell you they will be overjoyed and may even weep at your kindness. I've rarely had a person decline prayer.

If you responded with a 4-6, talk with God in prayer and tell Him you are willing, if He provides the need or opportunity. Then trust His timing and preparation. Be attentive to where He leads and when He prompts your spirit to pray with a woman He brings your way. You could even begin by simply texting a short prayer or scripture to a friend, or post a prayer for the day on social media.

If you responded with a 7-10, include this as one of your requests in prayer. Ask God to grow you in confidence in prayer so that you will be able to be a blessing to others in prayer. Be patient. Be persistent. Trust Him. He will answer this request with a resounding "Yes," I assure you.

When the idea of praying with another begins to stir an excitement in your spirit that outweighs the nauseous feeling, you will know that is your go-ahead to move forward and step out of the boat. May the God of peace equip

WEEK 5: SUPPLICATION, DAY 4

you with every good thing for doing His will, and may He work in you what is pleasing to Him, through Jesus Christ.²²

ASKING BIG FOR OTHERS

A multitude of books and guides are written on intercessory prayer. To intercede in prayer is to mediate, intervene, entreat, or make supplication on behalf of another. Often this type of prayer is done while those for whom we are interceding are not actually with us. However, intercessory prayer can definitely be made on behalf of another while that person is present. For example, Faith's prayer for Hannah was an intercessory prayer, because Faith was going to God on Hannah's behalf and asking for His help for Hannah.

We may not always personally know the people for whom God is asking us to pray. God has given us eyes to see and a heart that is moved by interests unique to each of us. We need to consider those outside of our immediate day-to-day. Are you willing to consider who they may be?

When your thoughts are on autopilot during the day, to what external influences do they tend to wander? Possibly you have an experience in your past which makes you particularly compassionate towards a particular group or segment in society. When you are running through social media feeds, what catches your eye and causes you to click down to learn more? Maybe your education or profession have given you authority or insights into a particular area. Whatever that interest, group, or area may be, this could be the focus of your intercession. God may be prompting you to pray for them.

The list of possibilities is endless but here are some ideas. Mark any that stand out to you, pique your interest, or pull at your heart.

☐ family	☐ friends	☐ neighbors	☐ teachers
☐ co-workers	☐ customers	☐ pastor	☐ clients
☐ prisoners	☐ homeless	☐ missionaries	☐ elderly
☐ local government	☐ federal government	☐ state government	☐ church
☐ civil servants	☐ law enforcement	☐ firefighters	☐ military
☐ economy	☐ education system	☐ librarian	☐ schools

MY VOICE, HIS HEART

☐ judges ☐ judicial system ☐ abortion ☐ child sex trafficking
☐ boss ☐ unemployed ☐ principles ☐ small business owners
☐ LGBTQ+ ☐ global slave trade ☐ elections ☐ the US President
☐ persecuted church in Middle East ☐ persecuted church in China
☐ persecuted Christians globally
☐ specific people or groups around the world who have never heard of Jesus

If you think of a group that is missing from this list, that is a green, flashing light that God might be calling you to pray, with your unique insights and heart. What comes to mind?

☐ _____ ☐ _____ ☐ _____

I hope you are getting excited about intercessory prayer. It is a profound privilege to work in prayer with God to impact the lives of others. God calls us to love our neighbor as ourselves. In living this out, we should be praying for our neighbor—whomever that might be for us personally. Who would God have you consider as your neighbor? Maybe it is the person living right next door. Maybe it is a group living halfway around the world. What an amazing truth that God can connect our lives to theirs in a profoundly meaningful way through prayer.

Please close us in prayer. Today, make no request for yourself but instead petition God for someone you know or encounter in your daily life, then ask big again for any area or group you marked or personally listed above. Write out your prayer, being as specific as possible, knowing that God greatly rewards this type of selfless generosity. Then take a deep breath, relax, and voice your prayer before God. I will agree with an "amen."

CLOSING PRAYER

"_____
_____
_____
_____
_____. Amen."

WEEK 5: SUPPLICATION, DAY

DAY 5

Week 5: Supplication

OPENING PRAYER

"Your Word is beautiful, LORD. It awakens my spirit. It encourages my heart and strengthens me. It is a balm to my soul when I am weary and lightening to my step when I am courageous. Thank You for this week, Father. Teach me for today. Grow me for tomorrow. Transform me for Your glory. Amen."[23]

DEEP DESIRES

This is our last day on supplication. While writing each day throughout this study, I have become concerned about fine-tuning and clarifying principles. My desire is for you to fall deeply in love with God as you spend time with Him. Forgive me if an unclear principle or teaching causes you to stumble. Go to God's Word, study, ask God for discernment, press deeper, and never give up in prayer.

There is one point I want to talk with you further on for a moment: submitting our will in prayer to God's will. God has given us a will and we are not to abandon it and become a robot follower devoid of dreams and desires. Simply put, the highest longing of our heart must be delighting in Him. Our heart then becomes a heart like His, a heart from which healthy dreams and desires will flow.

Prayer is a beautiful dance between God's will and our own. His hand is always extended for us to enter the dance floor with Him, but we must accept and take hold of His hand with a willingness to engage. On the dance floor He is meant to lead, but His greatest pleasure is not in leading. Rather, His greatest pleasure is in His dance partner.

When I learned about the importance of submitting to God's will in prayer, I kind of overdid it. I ceased making requests that were driven by the desires of my heart and began simply deferring to asking for His will to be done in everything. LORD, I pray for Your will in my life. LORD, I pray for Your will in my marriage. LORD, I pray for Your will in the lives of my children. LORD,

MY VOICE, HIS HEART

I pray for Your will in my ministry. LORD, I pray for Your will in this nation. LORD, Your will, Your will, Your will.

I wanted His will in all things in my life and in the world around me. I knew His will was best. At one point in prayer, His gentle, still voice whispered to my spirit, "Yes, Cathy; but what do you want? Share your desires with Me. I want to hear what your heart is longing for. What do you want? Share that with Me."

Would you open your Bible to Psalm 37:4? Please write it below:

_____

_____

_____

According to this scripture, what does God want to give us as we press into relationship with Him?

A) Joy for our day   B) Nourishment for our spirit

C) The desires of our heart D) Love, peace, and hope

Some of us may need new desires because the old ones were harmful or hurtful. No problem; God will give us new desires that are not only good, but every bit as passionate as any we have had before, if not more so.

The desires God gives us are unique to us. Yes, He knows our desires, but He wants us to share them with Him. As I began sharing my desires with God in prayer, rather than simply praying "Your will" prayers, things happened in my heart. Some things I prayed for diminished in importance in my own eyes; in other areas I discovered desires I didn't know I had; and at some point I discovered that old desires which had been there before were simply no longer there. It was almost like looking at myself in the mirror and seeing that, without my knowing it, I had gotten a full heart make over.

As your desires change, wane, and heighten, you can know this wonderful truth: "For it is God who is working in you, enabling you both to desire and to work out His good purpose."[24] One of these new desires God worked in me

WEEK 5: SUPPLICATION, DAY 5

was to help other women. I have to tell you, this was a desire I simply had never had in my life and would never have chosen for myself.

We women are emotional, often catty with one another, filled with need, self-justifying, and often just plain difficult. I had always favored my brothers to my sisters. I preferred working with men my entire career. I dreaded having to manage teams that had more than one or two women in them because I knew how profoundly more arduous it was going to be. Yet here in my heart was this new desire to help women. What?

I began sharing this desire with God in prayer and He has indeed been true to His Word and has given me the desires of my heart. I had the privilege of being the Women's Ministry Director for ten years with my church. Through Let's Pray Today Ministries, our team of women authors have recorded interactive prayer CDs and MP3 downloads to help women learn to pray through life's challenges as they draw near to God in relationship. For the past eight years I have had the joy of doing radio every week with my two beautiful co-hosts on Love Talk Radio in central Texas.

And today God has given me the incredible privilege of writing this study on prayer and joining you as we seek Him together in this season. Let's enjoy the dance of our lives with our Heavenly Father and share our heart's desires as we submit to His lead.

THE GREATEST ASK

There are some things in scripture that upon reading seem unbelievable. Our understanding of God's love, grace, and mercy falls so short of the depths, height, and extent of their true reality. One such scripture that knocks me to the floor, pierces me to the core, and challenges me in belief is Romans 5:8.

> *"But God proves His own love for us
> in that while we were still sinners, Christ died for us!"*[25]

What did God prove?

☐ His power   ☐ His mighty plan   ☐ His righteousness   ☐ His love for us

MY VOICE, HIS HEART

When did He prove it?

☐ When we believed in Him and repented of our sin

☐ When we were innocent of wrongdoing

☐ While we were doing good works that were worthy in His sight

☐ While we were still sinners

How did God prove His love for us?

☐ He gave us His Word, the Bible

☐ He made a plan for our lives, to prosper us and not to harm us

☐ Christ died for us

☐ Christ came as the light of the world and revealed the ways of God and the truth of God

Love, grace, and mercy unite full force in this truth revealed to us in scripture. I adore the HCSB translation that more clearly conveys Paul's emphatic tone by adding an exclamation mark at the end of his proclamation. There is no question mark, no added comma with an attached caveat, and a full stop period just would not do. Few verses in scripture pack the life-changing power of Romans 5:8.

During our time together, we have acknowledged that there are reasons God might not honor or answer our prayers. However, there is one prayer request upon which He puts no restriction: the request of the sinner to receive eternal life through Jesus Christ. The worst person on planet earth, no matter how vile—whether murderer, adulterer, rapist, liar, sorcerer, idolater, you name it—no person is beyond the love of God through Jesus Christ. That is a glorious and sometimes hard truth to wrap our head and heart around.

We tend to stumble over the truth that no matter how good or selfless we try to be, without the salvation Christ offers, we are in the same boat as the worst person on planet earth. The greatest request we can ever make is for God to save us from the penalty of death we are under, and exchange our death sentence for eternal life through Jesus Christ.

WEEK 5: SUPPLICATION, DAY 5

When we make this request, we do not have to wonder about His answer; He always responds "Yes!" We do not have to wait for His answer; His response is immediate. We do not have to worry about His true acceptance of us; angels are celebrating in heaven as He fully adopts us into His family as His child, with all the rights of an heir.[26]

Our intimate relationship with God begins with this life-changing request. The acceptance of God's free gift of salvation is the famous first prayer of all believers. Every future prayer will flow out of this prayer. We live in God's grace as believers, because of the mercy we received as sinners, through the love of Christ Jesus as victors.

On Love Talk Radio, we close our one-hour program with the ABC's of salvation. I include them here for us. Whether you use it as a guide to pray for your eternal life for the first time today or it stands as a reminder and word of encouragement, I pray God's Holy Spirit would wash love, grace, and mercy across our hearts as we engage in these words together.

THE ABC'S OF SALVATION

A – Admit that you are a sinner.

Romans 3:23: "For all have sinned and fallen short of the glory of God."

B – Believe that Jesus Christ is God's one and only Son, and that he died on the cross and rose again on the third day to offer us the free gift of salvation.

John 3:16: "For God so loved the world that He gave His only Son, that whoever believes in Him should not perish, but have everlasting life."

C – Confess your faith in Jesus Christ!

Romans 10:9-10: "If you declare with your mouth, "Jesus is Lord" and believe in your heart that God raised him from the dead, you will be saved."

Amen!

In case you are struggling for words around this, I am going to close us in prayer in just a moment. If this is your first time to ask for salvation in prayer, I would love to celebrate with you and the angels in heaven. Email and let me know (cathy@letspraytoday.com).

Thank you, friend, for walking through this with me this week. You now know everything I do about spoken prayer. The key is to use what we have learned—get on that bike and take it for a joy ride over the mountains, through the valleys, and along every path in this life God has staked out for us.

Next week we are going to begin learning about listening. This is something I am not very good at, but it has made every difference in deepening my intimacy with God. My confidence, trust, and hope in Him have profoundly grown since I began including listening as part of prayer. I know the same will be true for you.

CLOSING PRAYER

"Oh, how You love me, Father! You did not shun me in my sin, turn from me in my ignorance, or abandon me unto death. I was lost but You determined I would not be a lost cause. Your winsome love pursued me and proved to me Your love.

You sent Your Son Jesus Christ to pay the penalty for my sin that I could not pay. Jesus died for me the death of those who are cursed, death on a cross. By Your Holy Spirit, You raised Him from the grave to life, and He sits with You now at Your right hand interceding for me, His beloved.

Father God, I am a sinner who deserves nothing but is asking for everything. I confess I need a Savior, and that Savior is Jesus, the only name under heaven by which man can be saved. I repent and turn from my sin and turn to You.

I thank You for Your complete forgiveness, and I accept Your free gift of eternal life. I receive Your Holy Spirit into my heart to teach, counsel, and empower me to live the transformed life You have made possible for me. I Thank You for Your Son, for Your Holy Spirit, and for You, my Father in heaven. In the name of Jesus my Savior, amen."[27]

"Get into the habit of saying, 'Speak, Lord,' and life will become a romance."
OSWALD CHAMBERS

"Love the LORD your God, listen to His voice, and hold fast to Him."
DEUTERONOMY 30:20A

Week Six

WEEK 6: LISTENING, DAY

DAY 1

Week 6: Listening

OPENING PRAYER

"Gracious Father, I desperately desire to be near to You, living in the center of Your will for my life. My spirit is dull and my ears are untrained. You tell me that in my weakness, You are strong. You tell me that when I draw near to You, You will draw near to me. You tell me that in listening to You, I will find life. This I seek, LORD: my life in You, in fullness of joy and richness of faith. Forgive my stumbling, rouse me from my sleep, and awaken my spirit. I fix my eyes on You, LORD. In Jesus' saving name I pray. Amen."[1]

READY. SET. LISTEN.

We begin our last week together. Well done! I hope you've enjoyed it as much as I have. I pray you have grown in awareness and intimacy with God through every page, every day, and every prayer. May He bless this week with a double portion of joy as we seek to listen to Him in prayer. Let's approach each day with the expectation of receiving a personal word from our personal God.

Jesus often spoke in unusual contradictions: "The first will be last;"[2] "The least is the greatest;"[3] "Whoever seeks to save his life will lose it but whoever loses his life for my sake will find it."[4] During my time spent in quiet listening, I joke silently with Him that He left out one paradox: The easiest part of prayer is the hardest.

Friend, you will be tempted to get up and get on with your day as soon as you utter "Amen." Please hear this and take it to heart: Don't miss this time with God. If we are going to ask our Heavenly Father to keep us from temptation, let's start by asking Him to keep us from the temptation of ending our prayer time before we quietly listen in the stillness of our moments together with Him.

MY VOICE, HIS HEART

Over the years, women have told me: I cannot discern God's voice; I don't have that gift; God no longer speaks to man; I don't need to hear from God because I have my Bible; and other misconceptions and stinky beliefs. My heart breaks over what these beautiful daughters of God are forfeiting. We are going to unearth together a priceless pearl of wisdom in scripture where we are emphatically told that God desires to speak to each of His daughters, and has given us all spiritual ears to hear.

There are six accounts in the Gospel books of Matthew, Mark, and Luke where Jesus calls out, "He who has ears, let him hear."[5] Last time I checked, everyone has ears. Jesus' message was for everyone. They had to make a choice to stop and listen, desire to hear, and seek to understand. We have to make that same choice.

Now before we exclude ourselves from this by claiming Jesus was speaking only of those who could audibly hear His physical voice in those days 2000 years ago, let's jump across to the book of Revelation. Would you please go there and look up the following verses? Fill in the blanks below as you go.

Revelation 2:7
Whoever has ears, let them hear what the _____ says to the _____.

Revelation 2:11
Whoever has ears, let them hear what the _____ says to the _____.

Revelation 2:17
Whoever has ears, let them hear what the _____ says to the _____.

Revelation 2:29
Whoever has ears, let them hear what the _____ says to the _____.

WEEK 6: LISTENING, DAY 1

Revelation 3:6

Whoever has ears, let them hear what the _____ says to the _____.

Revelation 3:13

Whoever has ears, let them hear what the _____ says to the _____.

Revelation 3:22

Whoever has ears, let them hear what the _____ says to the _____.

Christ is speaking to the church, the body of believers, not to an empty church building. *Whoever* is a personal subject pronoun. It cannot refer to an object, such as a church building. *Whoever* refers to both singular persons—he and she—as well as plural persons—they. That is, "whoever" refers to both the individual believer as well as the church body as a whole. If you are a believer, you are part of Christ's church.

Because Christ calls us into fellowship together, we are exactly where He would have us be, among a fellowship of believers, corporately gathered, and often in a physical location we generally refer to as church. The *church* in this scripture also does not refer to church leadership exclusively. While it certainly includes the leadership, Christ is addressing every individual believer in these passages.

The Book of Revelation was given by Christ Himself to the Apostle John for every single believer that would live between John's day 2000 years ago and the day of Christ's return, which has not yet occurred. Friend, that scripture specifically says the Spirit is speaking in the days we live in.

Today, every single believer has something that only a handful of God's people in the Old Testament ever had the joy of experiencing, and that is the indwelling of God's Holy Spirit. We have the privilege each day of expecting a personal word from God. Because the Holy Spirit is living inside us, He can speak directly to our hearts and direct the thoughts of our minds.[6]

MY VOICE, HIS HEART

The Spirit of God is speaking to us today. Will we have ears to hear? Will we choose to stop and listen, desire to hear, and seek to understand?

STOP AND LISTEN

"Let the wise listen."[7] King Solomon was the wisest man to ever live. We can find his teachings on wisdom in the books of Proverbs and Ecclesiastes. Solomon writes that there is a time for everything under heaven, and more specifically that "there is a time to keep silent and a time to speak."[8] Here's the catch: In order to listen we must quiet our minds and stop all our busyness. We must stop with all the this and that, or as my mom calls it, needless putzing here and there.

Being about God's work is an awesome privilege, but we cannot pursue the work at the expense of the relationship. It may be easier to stop when we can see the person standing right in front of us; but even then, we can still miss the moment with our busyness. Thank heaven God does not condemn us but gives us examples of others who should have known better and who miserably missed the mark by pursuing a good work rather than recognizing the moment to stop and listen.

Let's open our Bibles to the book of Matthew and read chapter 17, verses 1-8.

1. Who was not seen by Peter but was unequivocally present?

☐ Abraham ☐ The other nine disciples ☐ Moses & Elijah ☐ Father God

2. What does Peter see?

☐ Jesus transfigured from His physical form to His spiritual form
☐ Moses & Elijah talking with Jesus
☐ James and John standing near Peter
☐ All the above

3. What does Peter fail to do?

☐ Get excited ☐ Let his thoughts run down a to-do list
☐ Take action ☐ Stop and listen

WEEK 6: LISTENING, DAY 1

4. What does Peter do?

☐ Focuses on the circumstances rather than on what is being spoken

☐ Interrupts what is being spoken

☐ Speaks up about his opinion on the situation

☐ Offers to make three tents for Jesus, Moses & Elijah

☐ All the above

5. Who interrupts Peter to stop his busyness and tell him to listen?

☐ Jesus   ☐ James & John   ☐ Moses & Elijah   ☐ Father God

6. Why does Peter respond with fear to God's voice?

☐ He did not realize God was present.

☐ He knew he had responded poorly by not listening in quiet humility.

☐ He had never heard God's voice before and it shook him to his core.

☐ He did not expect God to ever speak directly to him.

☐ Cathy thinks it's all the above but scripture doesn't specifically say.

I often think that if I could see Jesus face to face, listening would be so much easier. Friend, Jesus was face to face with Peter, and Peter still struggled to stop and listen. Let us never use not being able to see Jesus with our eyes as an excuse to not listen. Let's learn from Peter's experience and be aware that God is present and will speak to us personally. We simply need to stop and listen.

As we close in prayer today, we're going to spend time listening. We will listen with the awareness that God is present, even though we do not see Him, and that He is speaking to us through His Holy Spirit. We will simply be still for five minutes. Take longer if you like. When we're done, we will write down any impressions, stirrings, words, scripture, or the like that seem to gently press or filter into our heart and mind without our searching or grasping for them.

You may notice a gentle sense of calm, peace, or joy. In my experience, the Holy Spirit moves in personal prayer more as a fresh spring flowing in,

MY VOICE, HIS HEART

rather than a torrential flood pouring down. Your experience may be slightly different. We will discuss discerning God's voice later in the week. For now, we will be aware and attentive as we stop and listen.

> "Listen, listen to Me, and eat what is good, and you will delight in the richest of fare. Give ear and come to Me; listen, that you may live."
> Isaiah 55:2b

"I will exalt You, my God and King; I will bless Your name for ever and ever. Your greatness is unsearchable, and Your works are wonderful. You, LORD, are gracious and compassionate, slow to anger, and great in lovingkindness. You, Father, are good to all. Your tender mercies are over all Your works. You, LORD, uphold those who are falling, and You raise up those who are bowed down.[9]
[*Present any words of thanks or requests you have.*]
Father, attune my ear to Your voice, and my spirit to Your presence. I am listening, Father. In Jesus' name I bring these words of prayer and petition. Amen."[10]

Listening: Impressions, stirrings, words, scripture...

_____

_____

_____

_____

_____

_____

WEEK 6: LISTENING, DAY

DAY 2

Week 6: Listening

OPENING PRAYER

Would you please pen and voice a prayer to open us today?

"_____

_____

_____

_____

_____

_____, Amen."

DESIRE TO HEAR

> "Here I am! I stand at the door and knock. If anyone hears my voice and opens the door, I will come in and eat with that person, and they with me." Revelation 3:20

Several places in scripture we see God knocking on the heart of His children and waiting for a response before He continues with another word. We see Abraham, Jacob, and Moses open the door and say, "Here I am, LORD!"[11] Two similar heart knocks in particular are my favorites: the story of God calling Samuel, and that of God calling Isaiah. In the first, Samuel responds saying, "Speak, for Your servant is listening."[12] In the second, Isaiah responds, "Here I am Lord, send me!"[13]

Every word God speaks carries power and has purpose. If our hearts are bruised and our spirits are broken from living in the world of hard knocks, perhaps we need to respond to God's heart knocks and open the door to receive His healing words to mend us and His good purpose to rejuvenate us. While it may appear safer to remain busy and have someone else answer the

MY VOICE, HIS HEART

door, we will be the ones to miss out. Let's not be satisfied with listening to the words He speaks to others and not receiving any for ourselves. Let's open our Bibles and read Luke 10:38-42.

Who does it seem extended the invitation for Jesus to come to her door?
_____

Who remains busy and distracted when Jesus comes?_____

Who sets down her busyness and sits at Jesus feet?_____

What was she doing at Jesus feet? _____

When Mary chose to listen and Martha chose to keep busy, who was upset and complaining?_____

When Mary chose to listen and Martha chose to keep busy, who felt uncared for? _____

Who did Jesus say had chosen what is better? _____

Jesus told Martha, "You are worried and upset about many things, but few things are needed—or indeed only one." What do you think that "only one" thing might be? _____

Are you worried and upset about many things? If yes, what are those things that either right now or in general tend to make you worried and upset?
_____
_____
_____
_____

When we're worried and upset, we are not only easily distracted but we often cannot even focus or concentrate on what we need to do right now. We

WEEK 6: LISTENING, DAY 2

see Martha unable to focus on the task at hand and insisting on additional help. Listening to the LORD, with a desire to hear from Him, will help us focus our whole day. Our worries and upset emotions take many things away from us. They take our joy, our peace, our patience—they can even take our very life if we allow them. Let's make a point of bringing our worries and upset emotions to God in prayer so they do not distract us from listening or impede our desire to hear what God would say to us.

After Jesus gently corrects Martha, by responding that Mary chose what is better, He adds one unusually interesting point. What point is that?

_____

_____

What Mary gains as she sits listening will not be taken from her. The words of Jesus are eternal words, with eternal power and eternal purpose. If we stop and listen with the desire to hear, all we receive will be ours forever. While we cannot sit at Jesus' feet all day, it's a great place to start our day; and what He gives can't be taken from us.

One final point before we leave Martha and Mary to work out their sisterly differences. Who showed a measure of boldness in this scene we are witnessing? _____

When I first found this fun historical account of Martha and Mary in scripture, I thought Martha was the bold one. She invited Jesus into her home and then in front of everyone, she demands something from Him. Wow. Going to Jesus and asking for exactly what you want, that takes boldness. However, as I learned more about the context of this story in terms of culture, I realized Martha was being impatient and brash, not bold. Mary was the bold one.

According to the cultural norms of the time, women did not sit with men. Not only that, but they were not taught scripture, as they were considered beneath men and not worthy of such an education. I can hear the whispers from around the room as Mary walks over and sits down at Jesus feet: "What is she doing? Who is she to think she is worthy of such an honor?" Mary's desire to hear Jesus outweighed any notions of her lack of status or unworthiness. She let nothing stop her from hearing Jesus—that is boldness!

MY VOICE, HIS HEART

Let us not dismiss our desire to hear Him with false notions of humility. Let's not claim we aren't worthy of such an honor, or that we do not possess the spiritual maturity or discernment to distinguish His voice. My favorite pastor, whom I look forward to embracing one day in heaven, encouraged me to step into women's ministry when I felt wholly inadequate for the task. He used an analogy, asking, "How much faith is a child required to have in order to have enough faith to be saved?"

I was stumped at what, to me, seemed a deep theological question. He smiled, with a twinkle in his professor-like eyes, and responded with the answer: "All the faith that is required is, simply, all the faith the child has." If a child has enough faith to respond to the call of God's voice and be saved to eternal life, surely we have enough faith to simply sit at His feet and listen. Let's gather our faith, be bold, and listen with a desire to hear God speak.

> "Call to me and I will answer you, and I will *tell* you
> great and mighty things, which you do not know."
> Jeremiah 33:3 (emphasis mine)

When God speaks, we might be amazed as we seek to understand what He tells us. Scripture and attentiveness to His leading will help us in this. Tomorrow we will get into this further. For now, we will close in prayer and enjoy listening as we trust Him to give us the desire of our heart: to hear His gentle, loving voice.

INTERACTIVE PRAYER DOWNLOAD

If you are using the Let's Pray Today Ministries "Prayer for Beginners" mp3 download, go to Prayer #5 on track 6. Listen and pray all the way through to the end of Prayer #5 (approx. 7 minutes).

"Loving Father, You sit on Your heavenly throne, yet dwell in the hearts of men. This is too wonderful for me to fully grasp, but I believe with all the faith I have. Be quick to forgive my doubts, and guard my heart from double-mindedness.

Thank You that You do not leave me guessing and confused but confirm the words You speak to me through Your Word,

WEEK 6: LISTENING, DAY 2

Your Holy Spirit, and others. Teach me to order my days rightly. Please help me remove the obstacles and distractions that keep me from praying and listening. I thank You for what You are teaching me and what You are even now working in my heart.
My heart is Yours, Father. Make it Your own in every way. Dwell within me in fullness of joy and goodness. Amen."[14]

Listening: Impressions, stirrings, words, scripture...

_____

_____

_____

_____

_____

_____

_____

WEEK 6: LISTENING, DAY

DAY 3

Week 6: Listening

OPENING PRAYER

Would you please pen and voice a prayer to open us today?

"_____

_____

_____

_____

_____

_____. Amen."

SEEK TO UNDERSTAND

We have an incredible day ahead. Let's jump right into His Word together.

"Do not conform to the pattern of this world, but be transformed by the renewing of your mind. Then you will be able to test and approve what God's will is—his good, pleasing and perfect will." Romans 12:2

In this scripture, what are we to rely on to test and approve God's will?

_____

_____

What are we not to rely on to test and approve God's will? _____

_____

MY VOICE, HIS HEART

How is God's will described? _____, _____, and _____.

Pretend those three words did not exist in the English language. What similar words would you use to describe God's will? _____

_____

What do you think the world says we should use to test and approve God's will, or other spiritual matters of importance? _____

_____

As we seek to understand that which God would speak to us, we must use our minds first and foremost. The world, however, insists we must be guided by our heart and emotions. The world says, "What feels good and makes you happy is your personal truth and you can discover it through experience and experimentation. What feels right is right for you. Follow your heart and you will discover your true self and the way you should go." The world says everything is about us, that we are our own guide and our emotions are our best barometer.

I ignorantly applied these lies to my prayer life before I knew better. I went into prayer for the emotional rush it brought, and into listening for words of self-adulation. If that emotional rush didn't happen, I concluded God had not accepted my prayer or that the answer was no. This was horribly self-destructive. I walked away so often feeling inadequate in prayer, unacceptable to God, or doubting my own sincerity. This led to me becoming double-minded about my actual commitment to Christ and the relationship I claimed to desire.

Friend, I appeal to you, don't go down the road of seeking to understand with your emotions. Rather, seek to understand with the beautiful, capable mind God has given you. If you believe your mind is insufficient for the task, I have good news. God tells us, as believers and children of God, He has given us the mind of Christ.[15] We simply need to apply our minds rightly in accordance with God's Word and God's Holy Spirit. His Word instructs us to take every pretension that sets itself up against the knowledge of God and to take every thought captive and make it obedient to Christ.[16] That sounds like a tall order but we will learn to do both.

WEEK 6: LISTENING, DAY 3

God calls us not to be conformed to this world, but to be transformed. Conformity to the world is pretty easy to grasp and understand—and all too easy to do. What is transformation? The word used in this scripture for *transformed* is the same word used to describe Jesus' transfiguration. We looked at this together in Day 1 of this week. Paul is trying to make it clear to us that transformation is not something we can do on our own. It is the work of Christ in us, through the Holy Spirit. I have more good news for us, friend: These past six weeks, this is exactly the kind of work God has been doing in us! Everything God teaches us and speaks to us will be consistent with His work of transformation in us.

God's will is good, pleasing, and perfect. Everything our loving Father speaks to us will be consistent with His will. His words to us will be for our good, and will be pleasing when we understand them rightly. They will be perfect in their timing and purpose. God wants us to be able to examine, discern, and agree with His will for us. As followers of Christ, we do not become mindless robots; we become deep thinkers and determined examiners.

If this sounds too lofty for us, be assured, it is. When we ascend the hill of God, the right response is awe and wonder. We do not deserve this great favor. If we become overwhelmed, we can simply take a deep breath and call to mind the words God speaks to all who come to Him for refuge and strength: "Be still and know that I am God."[17]

KNOWING GOD'S CHARACTER, LOVING GOD'S CORRECTION

"All Scripture is breathed out by God and profitable for teaching, for reproof, for correction and for training in righteousness, so that the [wo]man of God may be complete, equipped for every good work."

2 Timothy 3:16-17

Do we truly desire to hear from God? Even if it means being corrected? The first name God gave for Himself is the name "I Am," which means the self-existent One. God is the only uncreated, eternal being. His character is unchanging. God does not evolve, develop, or adapt. This is why we can rely on Him in every circumstance. He is true to His Word and His Word is consistent and persistently unchanging, whether it be the word He spoke to Abraham three thousand years ago or His Word we hold in our hands every

MY VOICE, HIS HEART

time we pick up our Bibles. His Word and His character, revealed through Christ and the Holy Spirit, are One.

When the Bible teaches us that the fruit of the Spirit is love, patience, kindness, goodness, gentleness, and self-control,[18] we can know that each of those is a character of God. If God were describing His own character, He might say, "I AM patience, I AM kindness, I AM gentleness…" This is the likeness of character God intends for each of His children.

Wherever we may be falling short, God will work in us to transform us. Can we truthfully say, "I am patient, I am kind, I am gentle…?" If we aren't where we ought to be in one of these areas, that is something God may speak to us about. Do we have a desire to hear if it means hearing a word of correction? Let me assure you, God's correction is not like the punishment of man. The words we hear from God will not be mean, hurtful, or vindictive. While they will convict us that a change is needed, they will be gentle, loving, and kind words. If we hear a word that is cold, accusing, and mean, that is not God speaking. It is either self or the enemy.

Let's examine a standard our loving Father sets for correcting and speaking with others.

"Do not rebuke an older man but encourage him as you would a father, younger men as brothers, older women as mothers, younger women as sisters, in all purity." 1 Timothy 5:1-2

1. What do you think the root word for "rebuke" means? (Hint: this word is also translated "rebuke harshly.")

☐ Beat ☐ Chastise ☐ Strike
☐ Severely scold ☐ All the above

2. What do you think the root word for "encourage" means?

☐ Comfort ☐ Exhort ☐ Instruct
☐ Appeal to ☐ All the above

WEEK 6: LISTENING, DAY 3

3. How are we to treat older women, regardless of their sinful background or history?

☐ As women we are not really interested in

☐ As women who are unworthy but accepted

☐ As an estranged mother

☐ As our own dear mother

4. How are we to treat younger women, regardless of their sinful background or history?

☐ As ignorant outsiders who are barely worth our time

☐ As women who are unworthy but accepted

☐ As sisters who have disgraced the family

☐ As our own sister who has absolute purity

The answer to both 1 and 2 is "All the above." We are never to correct with words that beat down or cruelly chastise. We are to regard the woman as our own dearly beloved mother or sweetly innocent sister and correct with words that appeal, comfort, encourage, and instruct. If this is the standard God sets for us, we can be sure He fulfills that standard Himself.

There is a small scripture tucked away in the middle of the Psalms that reads, "One thing God has spoken, two things I have heard: Power belongs to you, God, and with you, LORD, is unfailing love."[19] I have a tendency to want to fix things, organize everything, and make details work out. In times of listening, God has often corrected me by reminding me that He is in charge, and the power to make everything work out right belongs to Him, not me.

As He speaks this in my spirit, every word is wrapped in gentleness, comfort, and encouragement. Even though He speaks one thing, I hear two. I hear that the power to make this work out rightly belongs to Him. But because He tells me this with love and gentleness, rather than as a harsh rebuke, I also hear that His love for me is unfailing.

Other times I have heard words like this: "You're such a nosy busybody. You always try to fix things but you always fail. You think you're Miss Perfect, but no one wants you involved here." Those words, my friend, are never from God. They don't line up with the standard He gives us in scripture, and they are not consistent with His loving, gentle character. We must take those words and throw them into the eternal trash heap from whence they came, allowing them to be burned up by fire, never to return for a second hearing. We are going to learn how to take lies and deceiving thoughts captive and make them obedient to Christ. We will demolish the lie, replace it with truth, and anchor it in scripture.

We approach this in a similar manner to what we have already learned in Day 3 of Week 3. In order to better hear the words God speaks to us, sometimes we need to identify and stop the torrent of lies we replay to ourselves.

- Begin by writing the lying words you are all too familiar with.
- Next, demolish the lie by writing in the truth. Speak the truth as you write it in.
- Finish by finding a scripture to anchor the truth and writing it in. Read the scripture aloud.

I believe our loving Father will use this exercise to bring transformation in our minds. We can use our Bible concordance or Biblegateway.com to help find the right scripture. If we are struggling to complete it, we can ask a mentor, group leader, pastor, or trusted friend for help. We cannot expect to hear God speak when we allow the words of the enemy to continue ringing in our ears.

I have started you out. Please complete a few of your own.

TRUTH	SCRIPTURE	LIE
God has blessed you with resources and a strong mind but you need to be discerning about where He is calling you to invest those blessings. Trust God and be still in those times and circumstances. He alone will enable you to work for His glory.	Proberbs 1:5 Let the wise listen and add to their learning, and let the discerning get guidance. Colossians 3:23a Whatever you do, work at it with all your heart, as working for the Lord	You always try to fix things but you always fail.

WEEK 6: LISTENING, DAY 3

TRUTH	SCRIPTURE	LIE
You are a child of God. He has called you to be faithful even when circumstances are difficult.	Phillippians 2:13 For it is God who works in you to will and to act in order to fulfill his good purpose.	You think you're Miss Perfect, but no one wants you involved here.
You care about people and what happens to them.	Psalm 112:4 Even in darkness light dawns for the upright, for those who are gracious and compassionate and righteous.	You're such a nosy busybody.

MY VOICE, HIS HEART

This may have been our longest day together yet. Forgive me if you are feeling some time pressure. Please do not skip this last exercise; complete it tomorrow if need be. You are a faithful daughter of the King! May God richly bless your perseverance in working through all of this with me. Please reflect on what you have learned today as we close in prayer. Make sure to spend time listening before you continue on with your day.

CLOSING PRAYER

"Gracious Father, I am never out of Your watchful eye. I praise You for Your loving and gentle character. I praise You for being a personal God who delights in having a relationship with me.
LORD, I confess that I feel overwhelmed by this truth. My mind cannot fathom how so great a God can be interested in a single person. Father, forgive me the doubting words that run through my mind. Forgive my unbelief and strengthen my belief. Thank You for Your loving patience with me.
Give me understanding as I consider the words You speak to me and seek to comprehend them. Give me discernment to separate Your words from my own. In Jesus' name, I reject the lies of the enemy that I have allowed to replay in my thoughts.
[Bring any lies that have replayed in your thoughts to God and confess the truthful words you now accept from Him.]
Teach me, LORD, to take every word that sets itself up against You and replace it with Your true and loving words to me. Give me a greater love for Your Son Jesus. I come before You and ask these things in His name. Amen."[20]

Listening: Impressions, stirrings, words, scripture...

_____

_____

_____

_____

_____

DAY 4

Week 6: Listening

OPENING PRAYER

Would you please pen and voice a prayer to open us today?

"_____

_____

_____

_____

_____

_____, Amen."

RECOGNIZING GOD'S VOICE

"Whoever is of God hears the words of God." John 8:47a

As we spend time in prayer and grow more intimate with God, we will come to more deeply know His character. The more we come to know His character, the easier it will be to trust and recognize His voice amidst the multitude of voices calling out to us every day on TV, magazine shelves, social media, and social circles. The more we are abiding in His Word and aligning our will to His, the clearer His voice will ring trustworthy and true in our ears.

Here are a few reliable guidelines I have learned over the years:

- God's every word to us will align with His Word in scripture.
- God will never speak a word to us which contradicts, overrides, or replaces His Word in scripture.
- God's voice convicts, but never condemns.
- God's voice is gentle, not harsh.

MY VOICE, HIS HEART

- God's voice is loving, not accusing.
- God's voice arouses joy and peace, not anxiety and self-loathing.
- God's voice teaches and corrects, but never belittles.
- God's voice says, "Take courage and fear not."
- God's voice never says, "Be discouraged and afraid."
- God's voice is life giving, not soul destroying.

RESPONDING TO GOD'S VOICE

Hearing God's voice is wonderful and life-changing. God's Word comes with power and purpose. We are responsible and accountable for how we respond. Look up the following scriptures and complete what is missing. If you do not have an ESV Bible, answers are provided in the Appendix (p. 229).

Isaiah 50:4b-5:
"Morning by morning He awakens me; He awakens my ear to _____ as those who are _____. The Lord God has _____ my ear; I have not been_____, I turned not backward."

Matthew 10:27:
"What I tell you in the dark, _____ in the _____, and what you hear whispered, _____ on the rooftops.

Luke 8:21:
"But [Jesus] answered them, "My mother and brothers are those who hear the _____ of God and _____ _____."

Hebrews 3:15:
"As it is said: "Today, if you hear His voice, do not _____ your _____ as you did in the _____."

WEEK 6: LISTENING, DAY 4

When I first began serving in women's ministry, I told my co-director that I would lead meetings, organize activities, and make business-related presentations to the church body; but I told her to never, ever expect me to speak on matters of faith.

My background was in managing large property openings. I had worked in three different countries for corporates like Fox Studios, Nike, and MGM. I was very comfortable speaking about project timelines, staffing levels, and budget needs. However, whenever I spoke in Bible study, or any group, about matters of faith, my voice got all wobbly on me and my eyes would tear up. I hated it and didn't understand it. So, I simply decided speaking on matters of faith was not meant for me.

We can make all sorts of decisions like this where we equate "difficult" with "not from God." We have to be aware, though, that when these decisions are out of line with scripture, it is not scripture that must change if we are to continue growing deeper in relationship with God. It is we who must be willing to change.

Which scripture on the previous page was my firm decision to not speak on matters of faith a direct afront against?

_____

The process of aligning my life to this scripture was hard, and at moments extremely embarrassing. I am forever grateful for the grace women have lavished on me over the years. I continue to press into Matthew 10:27 and marvel at what God does each time I persevere through the difficulty for His glory.

Now, 20 years later, I have emceed women's events, filled in for pastors on Sunday mornings, and I talk on matters of faith every week on Christian radio. My voice has become far more dependable and stronger as I have responded to His voice gently correcting me, telling me to take courage, and asking me to step into the work He has prepared for me. We must know this: We are not the only ones who ask. God also will ask us. He will not force or coerce. We can respond to Him with a no. But friend, say "Yes." Say *yes* every time. Our greatest adventures depend on our biggest yeses to God.

MY VOICE, HIS HEART

GOD RESPONDING TO US—
IN GOOD WAYS, IN GOOD TIME

There is a saying my wonderful friend B.K. taught me: "God is good all the time; and all the time God is good." We can take that to the bank and draw interest for eternity. You may be wondering why we have not focused once yet on answers to our prayers. We have touched on it several times, but have never drilled down. We will do that now.

I have found that specific answers to prayer are not nearly as important as I used to believe. God has done far more for me than I could ever have known to ask for. He has proven to me over and over that it is the abiding with Him through a life of prayer that avails much.

When Christ's disciples returned rejoicing because of the power and authority that they had in His name, Jesus responded to them, "Don't rejoice that the spirits submit to you, rejoice that your names are written in heaven."[21] Our abiding in prayer, more than our asking in prayer, results in far more provision, favor, and blessings than we could ever know.

Please hear me. I know the wonder and awesome rush of seeing a prayer miraculously answered. I also know the cries of our heart are serious matters.

As I finish this last week of our study together, I am at my parents' home in New Mexico because my dad was unexpectedly rushed to the hospital in severe respiratory distress and we weren't sure he was going to come out. I immediately got on a plane and headed down. You can bet we cried to God in prayer. We had every church prayer group we could reach do the same. I immediately texted my closest friends and asked them to join our family in prayer asking for my dad's life and recovery to health.

You can be assured I wanted a "Yes" from God—and right quick if He pleased. We were able to stand in this storm, not knowing the outcome, because we know our names are written in heaven. We have a certain and sure hope. We can trust our God knowing He is good all the time and all the time He is good.

WEEK 6: LISTENING, DAY 4

Scripture throughout the Bible gives clear examples of God answering the prayers of men and women. Sometimes He answers specifically as asked. Sometimes He answers in beautifully unique ways. Sometimes the answer comes even before the prayer is finished. Sometimes the answer comes years later.

My favorite accounts of answered prayer are in Genesis 24 (Abraham's servant), Judges (Gideon), 2 Kings (King Hezekiah), Nehemiah, Esther, and Daniel. I am partial to the Old Testament in understanding God's answers to prayer; however, the New Testament is just as rich and wonderful.

To every prayer, we can know that God will answer:
1. With a specific yes—with provision, favor, or blessing as requested;
2. Yes—but not in the way we requested or imagined;
3. No; or,
4. Wait.

The timing of His answer may be:
1. Yesterday—what we requested has already been provided but we are not aware of it yet;
2. Right away—the request is clearly and immediately provided for in one way or another, or an affirmation or reassurance of a firm 'no' is given;
3. In the near future—soon but not immediately so patience is required; or,
4. In the distant future—at some point beyond our horizon so perseverance is required.

An immediate "Yes" is what we typically think of as answered prayer, but God is so much larger and more faithful than that. Most challenging for me is discerning between a "No" and a "Wait." I have learned that if His answer is "No," He will close a door, slowly change my desire, or show me that my request was not in line with His best for me. If His answer is "Wait," a small door will remain open, my desire will remain or even grow stronger, and affirmation from scripture and other sources will generally come. We can trust that His "No" will be every bit as good for us as His "Yes."

MY VOICE, HIS HEART

Have you made a request that you don't believe God has ever answered? If so, please share it here. We will address this in our closing prayer.

_____

_____

_____

The substance of His answers have endless possibilities. Here are a few:

- Unexplainable miracle: Like manna from heaven or a lame man being instantly healed, there is no scientific or plausible explanation for the event.

- Mediated miracle: An outcome that is statistically improbable, but which has involved human intervention in some form.

- Scripture: A verse or passage from scripture clearly revealed during Bible study, scripture meditation, or any personal engagement with God's Word. Specifically answers a prayer request or affirms a word God spoke during listening.

- Personal provision: A physical answer to prayer at the hands of another person or group of persons.

- Personal affirmation or direction: A repeated affirmation or direction from two or more known sources—a pastor's message, a believing friend, one's spouse, and the like. Generally, to a private prayer request that has not been shared.

- Impersonal affirmation or direction: A repeated affirmation or direction from two or more unknown or unlikely sources—Christian talk radio, worship music, Christian books or other godly materials, a Christian conference or speaker, and the like.

- Orchestrated events: A series of unrelated events coalescing to provide an answer to prayer.

Our God is a God Who answers prayers. The answers take different forms and happen in His chosen and perfect timing, but He always answers. I am happy to report that after two weeks of praying, Dad is home and recovering. We are thankful and praising God for His favor. We must understand, however,

WEEK 6: LISTENING, DAY 4

that if the answer had been a "No," we would still have cause for praise, because God would be true to His Word to hold us firm, never abandoning or leaving us in the heartache.[22] Neither would He abandon Dad in death, but would greet him face to face with a home in heaven.[23]

As we close in prayer today, bring your outstanding request to God and ask Him to reveal His answer to you and, if needed, to encourage your spirit to persevere in prayer. If God's answer is "No" and you are struggling to accept it, ask Him to change your desire or to reveal the better plan He has for you.

CLOSING PRAYER

"Father, Your goodness surrounds me. All the time, You are good and You are good all the time. You never change. My hope is secure in You. You have called me Your child and adopted me as Your own. You will never abandon or forsake me. You are my Savior Who has delivered me from death and rescued me from the lies of the enemy.

In forgiveness You have restored me. In Your grace You have redeemed me. Your Spirit has taken this heart of stone and replaced it with a heart of flesh. You have revived and refreshed my soul. Thank You for Your many answers to my prayers. Forgive me for not recognizing them all. Open my eyes to them, Father. Strengthen me in patient and persevering prayer.

[*Include your outstanding request and other personal words of prayer.*]

All for your glory, forever and ever. Amen."[24]

Listening: Impressions, stirrings, words, scripture…

_____

_____

_____

_____

_____

DAY 5

Week 6: Listening

OPENING PRAYER

"Gracious LORD, You are the light of the world. You have said I am a child of the light. You have said I am a child of the day. You have placed me in this day and have made this day for Your good purpose. Awaken me, Father, and open my eyes. Awaken my spirit to Yours. Awaken me to Your presence. Open the eyes of my understanding to Your ways, that I may walk in them with gladness all of my days, for Your glory. May others see and know Your Son and His saving Name that is above every name. Amen."[25]

AWAKE & AWARE

"And do this, understanding the present time:
The hour has already come for you to wake up from your slumber,
because our salvation is nearer now
than when we first believed." Romans 13:11 (NIV)

Fireworks have been going off in my spirit this week. Our relationship with God is to be not only cherished but celebrated. One of the qualities I love about God is the many celebrations He proclaimed for His children. He intends for His children to remain awake and aware of His presence.

When we are in a deep sleep, we don't realize that we're in a false reality, disengaged from true life. When we are unaware that we are asleep, it's nearly impossible to wake ourselves up. We are also unable to tell fellow sleepers they are sleeping. We cannot enter their sleep, nor they ours. But there is no place inaccessible to God. I am praying, friend, that God is gently nudging our hearts, awakening our spirits, and opening our eyes. As the true Light of the world[26] shines on us, I pray His Spirit is awakening us to an awareness of His presence, His truth, and our true life in Him.

MY VOICE, HIS HEART

Please open your Bible to 1 Thessalonians 5:5 and write it here:

_____

_____

_____

At the very beginning of His Word, God makes it clear that He is the only One who can make light shine out of darkness. Before Him there was nothing and no other. In Him and through Him were all things made. Our true beginning is in Him and through Him. As He is the light that shines in the darkness, we, too, are meant to shine in the darkness. His Word tells us, "Those who look to Him are radiant!"[27] Friend, we have been looking to Him for the past six weeks. We are radiant. Our Father wants us to shine, not as a glaring distraction but as a glorious reflection of His Son.

ABIDING JOY

Every time I think of joy, I think of my dear friend Evelyn Davison and her JOY acrostic: Jesus Over You. The word joy is used over 240 times throughout the Bible. Joy means "glee, mirth, gladness, exceeding joy." God intends for us to be joyful. Fleeting happiness is not what He is about. He intends enduring, overflowing, life-changing joy. Joy is found in God's presence.[28] I love the New Living Translation of Psalm 40:4 that reads, "Oh, the joys of those who trust the LORD." If I could, I would add an exclamation mark.

The more we trust God, the more we will press into an intimate relationship with Him. We would never give a stranger the keys to our house. How then can we hope to give a stranger the keys to our heart? Here is crazy, brutal honesty: until now we have held onto certain keys. God has His hand out and is asking for all the keys, every single one. Will we surrender them to Him? Joy is ours in return—joy that rises up in our spirits as we abide with Christ. He alone will make the darkest places, wide open spaces.[29]

I want to share one of my favorite joy scriptures with you. Open your Bible to Psalm 16:11 and complete the missing elements:

WEEK 6: LISTENING, DAY 5

"You make known to me the _____ _____ _____; in your _____ there is fullness of _____; at your right hand are pleasures _____."

1. What does God make known to us?

☐ How to be happy
☐ Our frailties, shortcomings, and imperfections
☐ The right kind of work that will get us into heaven
☐ The path of life

2. Where can we get joy that is completely full?

☐ In a good quality chocolate bar
☐ In a fun night out with friends
☐ In a much-needed shopping trip
☐ In God's presence

3. What kind of pleasure does God offer us?

☐ Unending pleasures
☐ Pleasures that will not be taken from us
☐ Pleasures that bring eternal joy, rather than remorse and shame
☐ All the above

Nothing and no one but our Heavenly Father can fill us to overflowing with joy, and then go even further to offer us additional forevermore pleasures. No wonder we have a tendency to become joy junkies, focused on feeling our way through our faith. Let's guard our hearts against this tendency, friend, because it can quickly lead us to blindness.

Do you realize? The only people who spend their days feeling their way through life are blind people. They swing their sticks to and fro, feeling for what is around them; they have no idea if they are walking in darkness or light. I say this with full knowledge. My mother-in-law is completely blind. She lost her sight when she was in her late 30s. She is an amazing woman and has not allowed the loss of her sight to stop her from being a wonderful mother, grandmother, and wife. But I know if she had a choice, she would choose sight over blindness without a second's hesitation.

Let us neither choose blindness. Let's not go through life feeling our way, tapping our stick around hoping to hit on something that might bring us a temporary rush or fleeting happiness to make us feel alive for a short while. Let's not accept the lie that God is just a feeling experience and not a believing experience.

Let's neither buy the lie that being a follower of Christ is a boring, dull, and barely tolerable experience. Let's pursue an intimate, exciting relationship with God. When we spend time with God in prayer, let's look forward to a great adventure. Let's look ahead with great anticipation for today and tomorrow to be glory days.

This time with you has been a complete joy and overwhelming pleasure for me. Words cannot express my appreciation for the time you have invested in these pages and the faithfulness you have shown. I would love to hear from you and see your beautiful face. Key me a quick word and send me a picture if that would be something fun for you. It would be a delight for me.

I will leave you with this final word of encouragement, and will pray for you that you continue to press forward in loving intimacy and come to know more fully the all-surpassing greatness of our Mighty Father, God. He loves us more than we can imagine.

> *"What no eye has seen, what no ear has heard,*
> *and what no human mind has conceived—*
> *the things God has prepared*
> *for those who love him."*
> *1 Corinthians 2:9*

WEEK 6: LISTENING, DAY 5

CLOSING PRAYER

"Gracious Father, Whom have I in heaven but You? There is nothing on earth I desire besides You. My flesh and my heart may fail but You are the strength of my heart and my portion forever. You tell me I am valuable, I am capable, and I belong. I accept and trust You. Your Word is truth. I hand all my keys over to You and ask You to enter every room and space and fill them with Your light and abiding joy. Awaken me from my sleeping and make me fully aware of Your presence.
[*Share your own words as you finish your time in this study and press further into an intimate relationship with our gracious God.*]
I praise You and thank You. In Jesus' name, amen."[30]

Listening: Impressions, stirrings, words, scripture...

_____

_____

_____

_____

_____

ONE FINAL REQUEST:

Grab a journal and go back through the pages of this study noting the prayers you have written (they are beautiful!), the confessions you have poured out, the scriptures that worked deeply in your heart and mind, and the requests you have made. Make special note of the answers you have seen to your requests. Take a moment to praise and thank God for each one. Look at the wonderful work God has done as you have pressed into His heart these last six weeks! He will do even more day by day. Keep writing out your prayers and giving your unique voice to each one. Enjoy turning that plain old journal into an extraordinary prayer journal that chronicles the journey of a glorious daughter of God. Above all, continue using your voice in prayer as you press into relationship and experience God's heart and will for your precious life. God bless you, friend. ~Cathy

- ♡ Leader's Guide
- ♡ Week 1 Prayer True & False Review
- ♡ Week 2-6 Exercise Answers
- ♡ Bible Basics, Translations, and Selecting a Bible
- ♡ Prayer Styles and Formats
- ♡ Connecting to Prayer Groups in the US & Globally
- ♡ Favorite Books on Prayer
- ♡ Endnotes
- ♡ Acknowledgements

There's more...

APPENDIX

APPENDIX

LEADERS GUIDE

Thank you, friend, for stepping forward in this. May God richly bless your commitment to Him and the women you are leading. Below are a few suggestions to help you prepare. God has uniquely equipped you to make a profound difference in the lives of the women He is placing in your care. Above all else, enjoy them and the privilege He has placed before you.

1) If this is your first time leading a group, have fun surfing the web for ideas on how to be an effective Bible study group leader. Make note of any ideas that resonate or excite you about the privilege you are growing forward in. Share ideas with other leaders if you are doing this as part of a larger group.

2) Group time can be as structured or as informal as you choose. If you are doing this as part of a church-wide women's ministry, your leaders will likely have a format and guidelines already in place for you to step into. If you are leading a group in your home, keep it simple. This should be a joy and not a burden for you. Women are coming to be part of a meaningful community. They may enjoy coffee and snacks, but it is your smile and presence they are most looking forward to.

3) One request I personally have for each of the women is that before the six-week study concludes, each will open or close the group in prayer at least once. It is absolutely fine if ladies would like to prepare for this by writing out a prayer and reading it—as long as they do not give the prayer to someone else to read. One of our priorities is to become more comfortable with spoken prayer. This is exciting and wonderful. We will all show one another abundant grace as we grow together. I know this can be scary and if someone simply cannot voice a prayer in the group, we will show grace in this as well.

4) Be prepared in prayer. Prepare yourself in prayer to serve your group of ladies well. Pray for each member of your group by name, starting with yourself. Pray for love, wisdom, and joy to abound in private study times and group gatherings. Pray for the Holy Spirit to do His matchless work in each heart and mind. Pray for God to give insight and understanding into

MY VOICE, HIS HEART

His Word. Praise the Father for the unique voice He has given each of His daughters. Ask that He would give their voice strength and power as they seek Him and abide in His perfect will. Listen for any guidance He would whisper in your spirit as to how to pray, how to prepare, or what to focus on from the week's study in your next gathering. Record any guidance He provides.

5) Be prepared with material. Have discussion sections highlighted and be prepared to share your own experiences if others are hesitant to be the first to contribute.

6) Be welcoming. Welcome ladies with a smile and word of encouragement. Have some worship music playing softly in the background if possible, but turn it off before you begin.

7) Be on time. Begin on time, even if not everyone has quite made it yet. Welcome ladies who arrive late.

8) Be clear. Share your format with the group so they know what to expect during your time together. Open and close with prayer. Sharing prayer requests audibly generally takes more time than is available. Instead have ladies write out requests on note cards before class begins. These can be prayed over specifically by the leader or others in the group, and can more easily be followed up on in future weeks.

9) Be gentle. Never correct with harsh words. Trust the Holy Spirit to direct your ladies into all truth. Encourage and remind everyone that while we may have different experiences in prayer, our prayers should never be outside of God's character or contradict the truth of His Word.

10) Be thankful! Always thank ladies for sharing at the moment they contribute, no matter how big, small, insightful, or simple. You may be the only person this week to express gratitude to them directly. Always thank your ladies for coming and let them know how much it means to you that each of them made your gathering a priority.

APPENDIX

ANSWERS TO WEEKLY EXCERCISES

Week 1: Introduction

Week 1, Introduction, Day 2

<u>My Voice, His Heart: Prayer True & False Review</u>

1. Some people do not have the gift of prayer. FALSE.

Prayer is not identified in the scripture as a gift. It is not listed in the fruits of the spirit (Galatians 5:22) nor spiritual gifts (I Corinthians 1 and 12). Prayer is, rather, a spiritual privilege. Prayer is responding to the desire of the heart to communicate with one's Savior and Father. Prayer is our personal relationship with Christ in action. It is an active, engaged, two-way communication with the God Who created the universe and everything in it. Prayer can be a spontaneous joyful expression like Mary's or Moses' or Deborah's songs of praise (Luke 1:46; Exodus 15:1; Judges 1:3). Prayer can be a lament in the middle of the night when ill or sad (Psalm 6), or it can be a regular, daily discipline like Daniel's (Daniel 6:10).

Prayer can be long or short—just like any conversation. We cannot function without communication with others; neither can we function or grow spiritually without communication with our heavenly Father. Prayer is not reserved for a few; it is a spiritual need, an eternal blessing, and a divine discipline for all who have a personal relationship with God.

2. A good Christian must pray every day. FALSE.

In our fallen human nature, we tend to resist doing what we "must" do. Prayer is not meant to be a legalistic, ritualistic must that if we fall to accomplish, we spend our day feeling guilty. If we regard prayer in this way, we will not experience the joy of prayer in God's will. We need to be careful not to set up for ourselves a legal, rigid standard of a "good Christian" that results in guilt and shame if not flawlessly adhered to. This is a return to

MY VOICE, HIS HEART

Levitical and Mosaic law which we are not longer under if we are in Christ Jesus (Romans 6:14).

Luke 11 talks a lot about prayer and the parental relationship with our Father in heaven. Prayer is to be spontaneous, not regimented (v 9), persistent (v 10), and even impudent like a child or adult who just won't give up (v 8). Jesus often compared interaction with our Father in heaven to interactions with our earthly parents. When we pray, I imagine God feels something akin to the joy we feel when our children can't wait to share with us what is happening in their lives, both the joys and sorrows.

Examples of daily prayer abound in the Old Testament, and we see Jesus Himself going out in the morning to pray, and in the evening to have time alone with the Father. Friend, let us be with our Father in prayer like we would want our own children to be with us: spontaneous yet persistent, loving, expectant of the positive things that come from a parent's loving, patient, generous, and understanding heart. Let's persist in daily prayer not because of a rigid *must*, but because of a deep *longing* that nothing and no one else can satisfy.

3. In order to pray effectively we must bow our head and preferably be on our knees with our hands together. FALSE.

In Week 2, Day 3, Perfect Posture, we address what scripture says about posture in prayer and what the church has practiced through the years. Yes, Daniel did get on his knees before an open window when he was showing the satraps that their law could not stop him from praying to Yahweh (Daniel 6:10). However, King David prayed in bed and on his couch (Psalm 6:6); King Solomon stood with his hands raised in front of the temple (1 Kings 8:22), and Jesus prayed in public standing in front of a tomb (John 11:41). The point is this, friends: wherever you are, whatever you are doing, in whatever position your body is at any time, that's how you pray. Privately in your heart, aloud in private or in public—there is never a time or a bodily position that your Father will not hear you when you pray. James 4:8 says, "Draw near to God and He will draw near to you." No other conditions need exist.

4. If we pray throughout our day as we go, concerted daily prayer becomes less important. FALSE.

It is true that Paul counseled us to pray without ceasing (1 Thessalonians

APPENDIX

5:17). Keeping in an attitude of prayer with "abiding prayers" throughout the day is good. This can be compared to our children running in and out of our presence all day in short bursts: "Mom! Where's my skateboard?" "Mom! Thank you I found it!" "Mom! Jordan took my best shirt without asking!" "Mom! Where's the good snack bars?" "Mom! Thank you for making cookies!" We are glad to have these expressions from them. But to really grow and mature, our children need to participate in longer, more serious conversations with us.

It is much the same in our prayer relationship with God. Jesus is our example: Before making the critical decision of choosing the 12 apostles, Jesus prayed all night (Luke 6:12). At other times He withdrew by Himself to pray (Matthew 14:23; Mark 1:35). In Matthew 6:6, Jesus tells us to go to a private place by ourselves, close the door, and spend time in prayer to the Father. In Romans 12, Paul gives practical guidelines on how to live our faith each day and to be "be devoted to prayer." As we are 'in' the world, continuous acknowledgement of God's presence, power, and purpose keeps us from becoming 'of' the world. Taking the time to step away in order to pray and to listen to our loving Father helps us grow in our relationship and be refreshed in His love.

5. We should not pray when we are angry; we should wait until we have calmed down. FALSE.

God is neither condemning nor afraid of us when we are angry. Psalms 77 and 109 are written by a hurt, angry, and frustrated David. It is only after sharing these words honestly, that David is able to reconcile both his heart and will and turn them back to God. Job, chapters 7 and 30 highlight Job's words to God at the height of his despair. We can hear the anger and frustration in his words. Yet, God allows Job to speak all of his words, and then God answers, not in condemnation, but with mercy, grace, and ultimately with abundant blessing.

Ephesians 4:26 says "be angry and do not sin." Sometimes we are the most honest with ourselves when we are angry, as we do not take the time to be tactful. God is the best and most faithful Counselor to help us sort out the important stuff from the chaff at those times. He can lead us in truth and comfort us so that we are able to respond and engage truthfully with loving kindness and so avoid the damage that comes from speaking brashly to others in anger. James 1:6 tells us that "the anger of man does not produce the righteousness of God." Since when we are really angry, we will seldom produce anything righteous from that anger (no matter how justified we may feel at the time), praying at the time of anger and crying out to God can avert a major disaster with those around us.

6. If we do not sense God's presence while we're praying, we are likely out of touch with God and He is not listening. FALSE.

"Now faith is confidence in what we hope for and certainty of what we do not see" (Hebrews 11:1). If we could feel and sense God every time we prayed, would our prayers really require faith? Prayer cannot become about seeking a 'feeling' experience; it must be about seeking God and God alone. Prayer is one of the powerful intersections where the Holy Spirit engages front and center in the Christian life. Ephesians 6:18 tells us to pray "in the Spirit" on all occasions with all kinds of prayers and requests. Romans 8:26 encourages that even when "we do not know what we ought to pray for, the Spirit himself intercedes for us, with groans that words cannot express." Prayer is Holy Spirit territory.

We can know that the Holy Spirit will ignite, comfort, and embrace us in prayer like nothing we have ever imagined. As we experience the personal presence of God in prayer, of course we will desire that sense of closeness and communion every time – who wouldn't want that. But friend, we must guard against spiritual addictions and the tendency to have prayer become a 'feeling' experience. For once prayer becomes more about a spiritual high than an intimate relationship, we will be pursuing desires rather than God Himself. When we do not sense His presence, we can rely on the truth of His Word that when we draw near to Him, He will draw near to us (James 4:8).

7. The reason we have to pray is because we are commanded to by God. FALSE.

Recall when you first fell in love. You talked long hours when you were together just getting to know each other better. You talked on the phone even longer because you hardly could stand being away from each other. You told each other all about yourselves: your wants, dreams, hopes, and fears… but most of all you told each other in many different ways how much and how deeply you loved each other. You wanted to reveal all of yourself to this wonderful person, and you wanted him to do the same. No one made you talk

APPENDIX

to each other, you simply longed to be together. Love longs to communicate and share deeply.

Now, what if the only time your spouse, friends or children approached you was when they were commanded to do so by an authority figure? Would they be motivated by love or would they be motivated by the fear of disobedience? While fear of the Lord may be the beginning of wisdom (Proverbs 9:10), it is not the cornerstone of a deeply loving relationship. Jesus Christ is that cornerstone, and His love will supply our deepest longing and fuel our heart for Him. We never need pretend, but instead are free to be completely ourselves, the person God made us to be.

We are to pray on any occasion: happy, anxious, sad, in need, grateful, thankful; with all kinds of prayers and requests. We can proclaim like King David, "Because your love is better than life, my lips will glorify you" Psalm 63:3. God loves us more than we can ever imagine. He sent His Son to die so that we could live. Communication that is motivated by the deep longing of love, rather than the fear of disobedience, is the relationship in prayer He both desires and deserves.

8. We must only pray to God the Father and not Christ Jesus the Son; Jesus prays for us so we are not supposed to pray to Him. FALSE.

In prophecy of the coming Christ, Isaiah 9:6 reads, "For to us a child is born, to us a son is given, and the government will be on his shoulders. And he will be called Wonderful Counselor, Mighty God, Everlasting Father, Prince of Peace." Our (Mighty) God is Father (Everlasting Father), Son (Prince of Peace) and Holy Spirit (Wonderful Counselor). God is three separate persons, inseparable in unity, perfectly One.

We see "LORD" and "Lord" used in prayer throughout the Old Testament. In Matthew 22: 41-45, Jesus links the name LORD from the Old Testament to the promised Messiah, whom he reveals himself to be in Luke 4:21. "Lord" was also often used to refer to Jesus throughout the New Testament. Referring to himself, Jesus says, "Not everyone who says to me, 'Lord, Lord,' will enter the kingdom of heaven, but only the one who does the will of my Father who is in heaven" (Matthew 7:21). While Jesus Christ walked this earth with feet of flesh, thousands of people petitioned Him, talked with Him, and praised Him (Matt. 8:2-3, Mark 5: 22-24, Lu. 8:24, Jn. 11: 20-23). Is Jesus not alive today? Do we truly believe He is alive today? Why would we treat Him like an elephant in the room in prayer and refuse to address Him? No friend, we must not. We have the freedom to press into relationship with God, in His fullness, as much as our finite minds can possibly grasp and our human hearts can bear.

9. Prayer is meant to be easy and only less mature Christians really have to work at it. FALSE.

Mentioning this myth is a fun way to lighten the mood at conferences and seminars. I ask all the really mature Christians who don't have to work at prayer to raise their hands—in 15 years no one has yet. Jill Briscoe wrote a fabulous book in 2000 called "Prayer That Works." I remember being so excited to get my hands on it and learn all of her secrets. Through the lives of Elijah and Elisha, two men who were spiritual powerhouses and who saw miraculous answers to prayer, Jill challenged readers with the truth that prayer requires cultivation, surrender, and persistence every step of the way, no matter if you are a beginner or a spiritual giant. In Colossians 4:12-13, Paul commends a fellow Christian, Epiphras, for 'struggling' in his prayers, Paul extols his 'hard work' in prayer on behalf of others.

You see, prayer is not what is easy or hard; it is life that can be easy or hard. When life presents struggles, prayer will enter the struggle and persevere through it. When life is lifted to the heights, prayer soars to the heavens. Prayer is a privilege, a priority, a paramount joy. Prayer is guilt free, authentic communication with our Mighty God who loves us with a consuming love. Prayer flows from a heart full of love, sometimes from a heart full of sadness, fear, longing, desperation, or any other emotion we can experience in our complex and pressured lives. Prayer develops and deepens our relationship with God, from which our maturity comes.

10. Prayer is about lifting our requests to God, and is separate from our relationship with Him. FALSE.

I love this false statement because it provides a wonderful opportunity to better understand what prayer truly is. This study will address 'requests' in prayer in Week 5: Supplication. To better understand prayer, we might ask the following two questions. Are our conversations with our spouse separate from our relationship with him? Is our conversation with our children or our friends separate from our relationship with them? Not at

APPENDIX

all. These very conversations are the vehicles for the development of our relationships. The same God Who created the pattern for the development of earthly relationships through communication, patterned the same method for developing our relationship with Him.

We can see the intimate relationship Jesus intended for us by reading His prayers for us in John 17:20-26. Prayer is not just something Christians do, prayer flows from the very heart of who Christians are. We are able to make requests of God because we are in relationship with Him. Our prayers and requests flow out of that relationship, they can never be separate from it. If we find that we are only coming to God with our list of requests, we are certainly missing out on the deeper, loving relationship He offers. We would do well to press deeper into understanding what prayer holds for those who desire to experience intimacy with God. That, my friend, is what we are here for.

11. The more God loves you, the more He will answer your prayers. FALSE.

"The steadfast love of the LORD is from everlasting to everlasting" (Psalm 103:17). God's love is a complete, abiding love. His love is not a partial affection that can be measured on a scale or continuum. While His love is certainly what inclines His ear to the prayers of His children, His ear is never closed for lack of love.

His ear, however, can certainly be closed to our prayers, praises, and cries for help—not by His doing but by ours. The following is a list of reasons God may choose to close His ear to our voice or not move His hand to our request:

- Cherishing iniquity (immorality, injustice, sin) in one's heart – Psalm 66:18
- An unrepentant life engaged in iniquity (immorality, injustice, sin) – Isaiah 59:2; John 9:31
- Unrepentant wickedness, a man who plots evil – Proverbs 15:29
- Disregard of the cries of the poor – Proverbs 21:13
- Disregard for God's Word and instruction – Proverbs 28:9; Jeremiah 14:10-12; Proverbs 1:24-25
- Those engaged in bloodshed, injustice, and oppression – Isaiah 1:15-17

MY VOICE, HIS HEART

- Idol worshippers – Jeremiah 11:11-14
- Husbands that do not honor their wives - 1 Peter 3:7
- Wrong or selfish motives in prayer – James 4:3
- Double-mindedness (a mind divided between God and the world) and doubt - James 1:6-8
- Pride, Lack of humility – Amos 5:23 & James 3:6

The heart of God is overflowing with love for each of us – in an immeasurable supply. Our voice touches His heart as nothing else can. In Week 3: Confession, we are going to learn how to identify lies that are separating us from the truth of God's love and how to be quick in confessing and turning away from sin and leaning into His everlasting arms.

12. Morning prayer is far more effective than bedtime or evening prayer. FALSE.

Prayer is most effective, where and when prayer is most needed. We see multiple accounts in scripture of Jesus praying early in the morning, with crowds at midday, and by himself in late afternoon. Two of Jesus' most famous prayers occurred at different times of day. The Lord's Prayer in Matthew 6 and Luke 11 likely took place early afternoon in public. His prayer at the Garden of Gethsemane in Matthew 26 and Mark 14, occurred late in the evening in private. The key is that in order for us to be effective in prayer, we must actually engage in prayer. Thinking about prayer, reading about prayer, planning to pray, and listening and watching others pray is not actually engaging in prayer ourselves.

We must identify a time that is best for our schedules and natural bent. Are you an early morning person? Then praying in the morning will likely be best. Are you a night owl? Then set aside time in the evening hours for prayer. Is life simply a struggle right now? Then make time midday to stop, step away, and spend time with God to calm your heart and mind, and to focus your eyes on Him so you can see everything else rightly. You can do this friend. No one on the planet has more hours in a day than either of us do. I promise that the time we invest in relationship with our Mighty God, will never be counted as a loss, but will always result in a gain.

APPENDIX

Week 2, Adoration

Week 2, Adoration, Day 2

How long was this 'model' prayer Jesus provided? *4 sentences.*

Would you say the prayer Jesus provided was simple and easy to understand or complex and beyond the disciples' grasp? *Simple, yet richly profound.*

Is this the only prayer Jesus prayed in front of His disciples? *No, Jesus prayed several times in public, in the synagogue, and in front of His disciples.*

Is this the only time Jesus taught about prayer to His disciples and others? *Jesus taught on prayer several times in public, in the synagogue, and to His disciples.*

Week 2, Adoration, Day 3

Perfect Posture: Hands

Psalm 28:2: "Hear my cry for <u>mercy</u> as I call to you for <u>help</u>, as I lift up my <u>hands</u> toward your Most Holy Place."

Psalm 13:2: Lift up your <u>hands</u> in the sanctuary and <u>praise</u> the LORD.

Lamentations 2:19: Arise, <u>cry out</u> in the night, as the watches of the night begin; pour out your <u>heart</u> like water in the presence of the Lord. Lift up your <u>hands</u> to him for the lives of your children, who faint from hunger at every street corner.

1 Timothy 2:8: Therefore I want the men everywhere to pray, lifting up <u>holy hands</u> without anger or disputing.

1 Kings 8:22-23a: "Then Solomon <u>stood</u> before the altar of the Lord in front of the whole assembly of Israel, spread out his <u>hands toward heaven</u> (23) and said…"

MY VOICE, HIS HEART

Psalm 141:2: May my prayer be set before you like incense; may the <u>lifting</u> up of my <u>hands</u> be like the evening sacrifice.

Matthew 19:13: "Then people brought little children to Jesus for him to place his <u>hands</u> on them and <u>pray</u> for them.

Perfect Posture: Eyes

Psalm 123:1: "I <u>lift</u> up my <u>eyes</u> to you, to you who sit enthroned in heaven."

John 17:1a: After Jesus said this, he <u>looked toward heaven</u> and prayed

Perfect Posture: Legs

Mark 11:25: "And whenever you <u>stand</u> praying, if you have anything against anyone, forgive him, that your Father in heaven may also forgive you your trespasses.

1 Samuel 1:26: And she said to him, "Pardon me, my lord. As surely as you live, I am the woman who <u>stood</u> here beside you, praying to the LORD.

1 Chronicles 17:16: "Then King David went in and <u>sat</u> before the LORD, and he said: "Who am I, LORD God, and what is my family, that you have brought me this far?"

1 Kings 8:54: "When Solomon had <u>finished</u> all these prayers and supplications to the LORD, he <u>rose</u> from before the altar of the LORD, where he had been <u>kneeling</u> with his <u>hands spread out</u> toward <u>heaven</u>.

Ephesians 3:14: "For this reason I <u>kneel</u> before the Father."

Perfect Posture: Overall Posture in Times of Great Distress or Difficulty

Ezra 9:5b-6: "I ... fell on my <u>knees</u> with my <u>hands spread</u> out to the LORD my God and prayed: I am too ashamed and disgraced, my God, to <u>lift</u> up my <u>face</u> to you, because our sins are higher than our heads and our guilt has reached to the heavens."

APPENDIX

Matthew 25:39: "he [Jesus] fell with his face to the ground and prayed, "My Father, if it is possible, may this cup be taken from me. Yet not as I will, but as you will."

Based on the above scriptures, what did people generally do with their hands during prayer?
- *Hands were spread apart and held towards heaven*
- *Hands were placed on others if the prayer was for them*

Based on the above scriptures, what did people generally do with their eyes during prayer?
- *Eyes were often open and looking toward heaven*
- *Eyes were sometimes lowered or face was placed on the ground in times of great difficulty or disgrace*

Based on the above scriptures, what did people generally do with their legs during prayer?
- *Standing, sitting, and kneeling were all used in prayer*
- *Standing or kneeling with hands lifted to heaven while praying was common practice*
- *Prostrate on the ground in times of great difficulty or disgrace was not unusual*

Week 2, Adoration, Day 4

A Simple Expression: The Heart of the Matter (Luke 18:9-14)

"To some who were confident of their own righteousness and looked down on everyone else, Jesus told this parable: "Two men went up to the temple to pray, one a Pharisee and the other a tax collector. The Pharisee stood by himself and prayed: 'God, I thank you that I am not like other people—robbers, evildoers, adulterers—or even like this tax collector. I fast twice a week and give a tenth of all I get.'
"But the tax collector stood at a distance. He would not even look up to heaven, but beat his breast and said, 'God, have mercy on me, a sinner.'
"I tell you that this man, rather than the other, went home justified before God. For all those who exalt themselves will be humbled, and those who humble themselves will be exalted."

1. Where are both men praying?
At the temple

2. Are the men speaking their prayers or praying silently?
Both are speaking

3. Are they standing, kneeling, sitting or prostrate?
Both are standing

4. Are they looking heavenward or turning their faces down?
One is face up and the other is face down

5. How many words did the Pharisee pray?
All of these

6. How many words did the tax collector pray?
All of these

Week 3, Confession

Week 3, Confession, Day 1

Sweet Confessions

Ephesians 4:23-24: "to be made new in the attitude of your minds; and to put on the new self, created to be like God in true righteousness and holiness."

APPENDIX

Week 3, Confession, Day 3

What Binds Your Heart?

GOD'S GOODNESS

Truth	Scripture	Lie
God created all things, and all of creation is held together in Him.	Colossians 1:16-17	God is just a feel good, made up figment of imagination. This world is here by chance.
God is a loving Father who listens and cares for me personally.	Matthew 6:6 I Corinthians 6:18	God is not interested in me personally. He doesn't take time to listen to me.
God designed me wonderfully and purposefully.	Psalm 139:14-15	I am an accident, a freak of nature. My body and the way I look isn't good enough.
God has a plan for my life and desires good things for me.	Jeremiah 29:11	My life is pointless and no one cares what happens to me.

MY IDENTITY

Truth	Scripture	Lie
God accepts me and I am completely and fully loved by Him.	Romans 5:8 Ephesians 3:17-19	I have done too many bad things for God to want me; I have to be successful in order to be good enough for Him to love me.
I am chosen and adopted by God. I am His daughter.	John 15:16 Ephesians 1:4-5	I am a reject. I am abandoned and on my own. No one wants me.
There is nothing I have to fear.	2 Timothy 1:7 Isaiah 26:3 Philippians 4:6-7	I cannot escape fear and anxiety. I will never have peace.

Week 4, Thanksgiving

Week 4, Thanksgiving, Day 1

The Pessimist, the Optimist, and the Psalmist

"But my eyes are fixed on you, Sovereign LORD; in you I take refuge—do not give me over to death." Psalm 141:8 (NIV)

"My eyes are always on the LORD, for only He will release my feet from the snare." Psalm 25:15 (NIV)

"To You I lift up my eyes, oh You who are enthroned in the heavens." Psalm 123:1 (NIV)

"I keep my eyes always on the LORD. With Him at my right hand, I will not be shaken." Psalm 16:8 (NIV)

Week 4, Thanksgiving, Day 5

Jesus Cleanses Ten Lepers (Luke 17:11-19)

1. Who met Jesus? *Lepers.*
2. How many were there? *10.*
3. What did they ask Jesus for? *Mercy.*
4. How did Jesus respond? *Healing.*
5. How many returned to see Jesus again? *1.*
6. What was the purpose of returning to see Jesus? *Thanksgiving.*
7. What was Jesus' response? *He was amazed that only 1 returned to give thanks when all had received their request.*

APPENDIX

Week 5, Supplication

Week 5, Supplication, Day 1

A Promise Given (Philippians 4:6-7)

1. What does God say we should be anxious about? *Nothing.*

2. In regards to what, does God say we should go to Him with our requests? *Everything.*

3. What extra does God promise to give even though we didn't even ask for it? *Peace.*

4. What are the attributes of God's peace highlighted here? *All the above.*

A Steadfast Assurance

Psalm 107:6: Then they cried out to the LORD in their trouble, and he delivered them from their distress.

Jeremiah 33:3: Call to me and I will answer you and tell you great and unsearchable things you do not know.

Matthew 21:22: If you believe, you will receive whatever you ask for in prayer.

Luke 11:9-10: So I say to you: Ask and it will be given to you; seek and you will find; knock and the door will be opened to you. For everyone who asks receives; the one who seeks finds; and to the one who knocks, the door will be opened.

John 14:14: You may ask me for anything in my name, and I will do it.

John 15:7: If you remain in me and my words remain in you, ask whatever you wish, and it will be done for you.

Philippians 4:19: And my God will meet all your needs according to the riches of his glory in Christ Jesus.

James 1:5: If any of you lacks wisdom, you should ask God, who gives generously to all without finding fault, and it will be given to you.

Week 5, Supplication, Day 5

Deep Desires

According to Psalm 37:4, what does God want to give us as we press into relationship with Him? *The desires of our heart.*

The Greatest Ask (Romans 5:8)

What did God prove? *His love for us.*

When did He prove it? *While we were still sinners.*

How did God prove His love for us? *Christ died for us.*

Week 6, Listening

Week 6, Listening, Day 1

Ready. Set. Listen.

Revelation 2:7; 2:11; 2:29; 3:6; 3:13; and 3:22:
Whoever has ears, let them <u>hear</u> what the <u>Spirit</u> says to the <u>churches</u>.

Stop and Listen (Matthew 17:1-8)

1. Who was not seen by Peter but was unequivocally present? *Father God.*
2. What does Peter see? *All the above.*
3. What does Peter fail to do? *Stop & listen.*

APPENDIX

4. What does Peter do? *All the above.*

5. Who interrupts Peter to stop his busyness and tells him to listen? *Father God.*

6. Why does Peter respond with fear to God's voice? *Cathy thinks it is all of the above but scripture doesn't specifically tell us.*

Week 6, Listening, Day 2

<u>Jesus at the home of Martha and Mary (Luke 10:38-42)</u>

Who seems to be the one who extended the invitation for Jesus to come to her door? *Martha.*

Who remains busy and distracted when Jesus comes? *Martha.*

Who sets down her busyness and sits down at Jesus feet? *Mary.*

What was she doing at Jesus feet? *Listening to Him.*

When Mary chose to listen and Martha chose to keep busy, who was upset and complaining? *Martha.*

When Mary chose to listen and Martha chose to keep busy, who felt uncared for? *Martha.*

Who did Jesus say had chosen what is better? *Mary.*

What do you think that "only one" thing might be that Jesus is talking about? *Answers will vary: time with Jesus, listening to Jesus, Jesus being our priority over all others, etc.*

After Jesus gently corrects Martha by responding that Mary chose what is better, He adds on one unusually interesting point. What point is that? *It will not be taken from her.*

One final point before we leave Martha and Mary to work out their sisterly differences. Who showed a measure of boldness in this scene we are witnessing? *Mary.*

Week 6, Listening, Day 3

Seek to Understand (Romans 12:2)

In this scripture, what are we to rely on to test and approve God's will? *Our minds; our renewed minds.*

What are we not to rely on to test and approve God's will? *Patterns of the world.*

How is God's will described? *Good; pleasing & perfect.*

Consider the three words used to describe God's will. Pretend those words did not exist in the English language, what like words would you use to describe God's will? *Answers will vary.*

What do you think the world says we should use to test and approve God's will, or spiritual matters of importance? *Answers will vary.*

Knowing God's Character, Loving God's Correction

1. What do you think the root word for "rebuke" means? (Hint: this word is also translated "rebuke harshly.") *All the above.*

2. What do you think the root word for "encourage" means? *All the above.*

3. How are we to treat older women, regardless of their sinful background or history? *As our own dear mother.*

4. How are we to treat younger women, regardless of their sinful background or history? *As our own sister who has absolute purity.*

APPENDIX

Week 6, Listening, Day 4

Responding to God's Voice

Isaiah 50:4b-5: "Morning by morning He awakens; He awakens my ear to <u>hear</u> as those who are <u>taught</u>. The Lord God has <u>opened</u> my ear; I have not been <u>rebellious</u>, I turned not backward."

Matthew 10:27: "What I tell you in the dark, <u>say</u> in the <u>light</u>, and what you hear whispered, <u>proclaim</u> on the rooftops."

Luke 8:21: "But He [Jesus] answered them, "My mother and brothers are those who hear the <u>word</u> of God and <u>do</u> <u>it</u>."

Hebrews 3:15: "As it is said: 'Today, if you hear His voice, do not <u>harden</u> your <u>hearts</u> as you did in the <u>rebellion</u>.'"

Which scripture above was my firm decision a direct afront against? *Matthew 10:27*

Week 6, Listening, Day 5

Abiding Joy

Psalm 16:11:
"You make known to me the <u>path</u> <u>of</u> <u>life</u>; in your <u>presence</u> there is fullness of <u>joy</u>; at your right hand are pleasures <u>forevermore</u>."

1. What does God make known to us? *The path of life.*

2. Where can we get joy that is completely full? *In God's presence.*

3. What kind of pleasure does God offer us? *All of the above.*

BIBLE BASICS, TRANSLATIONS & SELECTING A BIBLE

By now you know many things about me, as I have endeavored to be as transparent with you as I can be. I want you to know my heart. I love the Word of God! I love the book that holds all those precious words from His heart to yours and mine. I love the feel of the pages, and the sound of them turning, and the smell of a new one after the old one is outlined and underlined and the binding is cracking and the cover is worn. I still use the old one with the new one just to see the underlined verses I love, and refresh myself with the notes I have written in it over the years of use, the prayers recorded for my children and my family, and the prayers answered and noted in the margins! As the years of study have piled up, so have my Bibles. So now I would like to share with you some of what I have learned about Bibles to use for Bible study.

Please know I am not a Bible expert or theologian. I am sharing what I have gleaned over the years of choosing and purchasing Bibles for myself and others. There is much more to know that is way beyond my limited scope of knowledge. If you find mistakes, just write me at cathy@letspraytoday.com. I would love to know you and know more about the Bibles we love. Okay, that said, here goes...

Basic Bible Information

The Bible is a composite of many books written by many different authors, all of whom have written the words that were inspired by the Holy Spirit, or "breathed out by God" (2 Timothy 3:16). There are 66 books in the Bible: 39 in the Old Testament and 27 in the New Testament. The Catholic Bible has more because it contains the Apocrypha, which is sandwiched between the Old Testament and the New Testament. The Apocrypha consists of seven major books and also some additions to the books of Esther and Daniel. The Catholic Church considers the Apocrypha to be Canon, that is, holy scripture. The books of the Apocrypha are regarded as wisdom and history by Protestants, and are well worth knowing, but they aren't considered to be Canon. How the theologians decided all that is more than can be covered here, but those are the basics.

APPENDIX

Any Bible as described above is useful for this Bible study on prayer. The citations referenced in this study can be found accurately in any of them. The books always appear in the same order in every Bible. A list of all the books in order can be found on one of the first few pages in any Bible. This will help you locate scripture as you are getting used to where everything is found. Soon you will have the books memorized and will find yourself flipping easily to your favorite scriptures. Keep at it. The rewards are great!

Bible Translations

There are a few different methods of translating the Bible. The literal method, or formal equivalence, attempts to be true to the exact words and phrases of the original languages found in the original manuscripts, basically the Hebrew (Old Testament) and the Greek (New Testament). The literal translations are a little more difficult to understand, but are worth the effort and many people love them. They are called word-for-word translations. Examples of these are the King James Version (KJV), which for me is the hardest to understand because of archaic words, the more readable New King James Version (NKJV), the Modern English Version (MEV), the Revised Standard Version, the New American Standard Bible (NASB), and the English Standard Version ESV. These are especially good in Bible study when you are wanting to look up the meanings of specific words and see how they are used in other places in the Bible.

The next method of translation is called dynamic equivalency, or a thought-for-thought translation. Along with modern methods in archaeology and linguistics has come more in-depth knowledge of the meanings of the words and idiom of the original languages. Therefore, we can read in these translations not only what the words say, but what they mean in an updated context. Optimal Equivalence is when the text is true to the literal translation when there is no problem translating the text into modern English, but uses a dynamic approach as well to attempt to convey to the modern reader the same understanding of the words an ancient reader would have when reading the original texts. Examples of these are the New International Version (NIV), the Holman Christian Standard Bible (HCSB), the Christian Standard Bible (CSB), the New American Bible Revised Edition (NABRE), and the New Living Translation (NLT).

Last, there are the paraphrased editions of the Bible. These have the primary goal of conveying the messages in the Bible in a simple, easily understood manner. The weakness in this method is that it is not really good for serious Bible study. The strength in this method is that it can be understood by very young children and is good for Bible stories and family devotions where there are young listeners. Examples of these are the Message (MSG), the New International Reader's Version (NIrV), The Living Bible (TLB), The Passion Translation (TPT), and the Contemporary English Version (CEV).

There are more Bibles in each category than those I have listed here. I have listed the ones with which I am familiar, but this is far from an exhaustive list. My personal favorites are the NASB, the Amplified Bible, and the HCSB for a specific reason: they capitalize the pronouns when referring to God: He, You, etc. I know there are some scholarly arguments for not capitalizing pronouns, but they have never been convincing to me. However, I really like the NIV and the NLT because they are so readable, and I use them very often though they do not capitalize the pronouns...but they are not my favorites.

The point of saying all this is that you will also have your favorites, and they may not be the same as mine, and that is just the wonder of our many differences. I love differences...have you ever tried to count the many different shades of green in a forest or glen? I think God loves differences too, He made so many of them... Ahh, back to Bibles.

Types of Bibles

The many different translations of the Bible also come in different types. The simplest form of Bible is text only. In addition to the text there are a minimum of footnotes that are mostly translation related. Some of these text-only Bibles come with the words spoken by Christ printed in red, and that will be specified on the box or cover in which the Bible is sold. These also can be purchased in large and giant print. There are also parallel Bibles, which have the text of two to four different translations placed side by side so you can compare and contrast the different translations of the text.

The next type is the reference Bible. This Bible contains the text, and also has center-column or end-of-verse references that list the other places in the Bible that refer to the same word or thought as is in that verse. Reference Bibles also have a concordance, which is like a dictionary, listing key words

APPENDIX

alphabetically along with popular verses that contain the same word. The concordance is located at the back. Reference Bibles may also have maps that show the Biblical lands and where many ancient places were located. All of this additional information takes up very little additional room, so you will have a Bible that is good for reading and for study that is not bulky and can easily fit inside a medium-sized purse. These also can have the words of Christ in red. You will find all of what is inside a Bible listed on the box in which it comes.

Study Bibles—these are wonderful! A huge handful of Bible, but with a ton of biblical information at your fingertips. In my experience, these are of two general types: scholarly, and application. All Study Bibles have copious teaching notes, usually at the bottom part of the page, that can include archeological information, scholarly information, scripture application to your own life, and more. The newer editions contain color photos and maps of the places about which you are reading on the same page as the verses. There are also introductions to each book of the Bible, often outlines of the book, information about the author, and the date it was written. There are usually charts and articles about key people or subjects; in short, a ton of information. Many of the same study Bibles come in several different translations, so you can pick your favorite and almost have a seminary at your fingertips.

The Life Application Study Bible is probably one of the most popular. It is my first choice for new Christians, as it teaches how to apply the scripture to one's life.

The ESV Study Bible is probably the most scholarly of the literal versions; the NASB Study Bible is another literal translation with the same type of scholarly notes as in the NIV Study Bible. The Thompson Chain Study Bible has the very best of topical study notes. The New Inductive Study Bible teaches you to study the Bible for yourself, with excellent study guides and charts and helps. The Key Word Study Bible is great for studying the meanings of specific words, as it has key Hebrew and Greek words underlined and linked to Strong's concordance, which is included in the Bible.

There are pastoral Study Bibles by popular biblical scholars, such as the MacArthur Study Bible (John MacArthur) and the Jeremiah Study Bible (David Jeremiah).

There are specific focuses in some Study Bibles: the Chronological Study Bible, the Archeological Study Bible, the Apologetics Study Bible, Women's Study Bibles, Couples Study Bibles, and more.

Choosing your own special Bible: This is the easiest part of this section for me to write. It is so simple. Trust yourself and how God leads you. Go to your local Christian bookstore so you can look and read and see for yourself. Pray about it. You will find one specific Bible that you love. Whether it is text or reference or study or pastoral, you will know it when you open it and read. Read from the different translations, look at the different types of study Bibles, take time to read some of the notes. You will find one that exactly fits you. The Bible is God's love letter to all of us. In it is the road map for our lives. The Bible teaches us how to pray, and how to love Him, ourselves, and each other more fully—which is, of course, our goal.

PRAYER STYLES AND FORMATS

You may hear people talking about different types of prayer. Do not feel overwhelmed. I am listing for you here a number of different types of prayer to help you build your understanding. You might even want to try a few out for yourself.

<u>Prayer Walking</u>
Prayer Walking is intercessory rather than personal devotional prayer and is generally done in a low-profile manner. It is sometimes referred to as praying on-site with insight.

Usually, teams of two will pray over a specific area as they walk together. The area covered is typically a circumference surrounding a key location where God is being sought to work in His power and might. For example, moms might walk around the school campus while praying for God to address specific issues facing the schoolboard, administration, staff, or students. Neighbors might walk around their neighborhood praying for God to save marriages, uncover abuse and depression, and save each family on the block.

Prayer walking an area can be a one-time event, but usually it is an ongoing activity. The more one perseveres, the more the Holy Spirit will give insight into the realities and needs to bring forward in prayer. There is no place

APPENDIX

off limits to this wonderful form of prayer. I have joined a group on a virtual prayer walk around Washington DC where a pastor had his phone and everyone connected via Facebook—it was awesome to hear God prompt prayers in each of us as the pastor walked past the Supreme Court, Capitol Building, White House, and other landmarks where critical decisions for the nation take place.

It is key to remember that the goal of prayer walking is quiet, attentive prayer, not making a spectacle of prayer. We want to remain largely unnoticed by those coming and going.

Prayer Flights

This is the same principle as prayer walking but in an airplane. During the National Day of Prayer each year, volunteer pilots pray over the USA from coast to coast and border to border. What an incredible privilege.

Popcorn Prayer

Ideal for group prayer in which each member is expected to participate and the burden of length or eloquence in prayer is removed. The leader opens the prayer and introduces a topic or prayer element the group is to pray around. Each person, in no particular order, prays between one word to one sentence only. Group members can pray multiple times on the specific topic or element in these short, focused prayers.

When no more prayers are being added, or when the allotted time for the specific element has passed, the leader gently transitions the group to the next topic or element and the popcorn prayer continues. The leader or a designated person closes the prayer when the time for the gathering has ended. The ACTS prayer model is well-suited for this type of group prayer.

Guided Prayer

Guided Prayer can be used for both individuals or groups, and for both private or public settings. This is prayer that uses a prepared outline, which generally includes topics, scripture, and key prayer points related to each topic. Thousands of prayer guides are put out every year by a multitude of different ministries. No matter what you want to pray for, there's a good chance a prayer guide has been designed to help you pray for it.

MY VOICE, HIS HEART

If you are going to organize a group prayer time for your church, group, or gathering, you will likely put together some sort of a guide to get everyone on the same page to cover the prayer needs in unity and like-minded direction. Guided prayer can also be combined with prayer walking when large groups are coming together to cover an area in prayer. The National Day of Prayer Task Force often organizes guided prayer walks at all the state capitols each year on the first Thursday in May.

Declarative Prayer
This type of prayer can be abused and misunderstood as a "name it and claim it" approach to prayer. However, Declarative Prayer is not about fulfilling personal desire; it is focused on God's will and where we see the Holy Spirit working. Unlike prayer that petitions and requests, this type of prayer declares what has already been given. Declarative prayer should be anchored in God's Word.

While petitioning prayer may be voiced like this: "LORD, Your Word says You have given me the mind of Christ. Please help me to take my anxious thoughts captive and place my trust firmly in You and stop worrying over these issues that I know You are sovereign over." Declarative prayer may, on the same issue, be voiced like this: "LORD, You have said that You have not given me a spirit of fear, but of power and of love and of a sound mind. You have given me the very mind of Christ. Therefore, I declare that worry will not consume my thoughts and fear will not reign over my mind; instead, power and love will be my mantle and my mind will be soundly fixed on the eternal goodness of God."

Declarative Prayer is also often used in intercessory prayer. I tend to use a greater measure of petitionary prayer in my personal prayer time and declarative prayer when I am prayer walking.

Group Prayer
Based on the "two or more" principle found in Matthew 18:20, group prayer is a wonderful option for a new believer who wants to learn and grow in prayer with more experienced believers. God promises to be in the midst of people when they are gathered together in His name. I have found that there is something exceptional about group prayer that fills participants with a pervasive sense of persevering hope, whether they initially come together in exhaustion and desperation or excitement and joy.

APPENDIX

Topical Prayer
Often groups or organizations have themes or topics to organize their prayer times or prayer schedules. It is not as detailed as a prayer guide. Topical prayer serves the purpose of unifying the prayers of many and focusing those unified prayers towards a specific group, need, or area of concern. You might organize with a group of friends to pray for your husbands on Monday, children on Tuesday, neighbors on Wednesday, each other on Thursday, a particular seeker or lost individual on Friday, and extended family on Saturday. There are infinite options here.

Praying Psalms
This is a great fall back if you are ever at a loss for words but want to spend time in prayer. As many of the Psalms were written by King David, who is called "a man after God's own heart," you can't go wrong by using your voice to bring these words before God's throne. There are Bible studies written specifically on praying the Psalms; there is music you can download to pray with; or you can simply begin at Psalm 1 and pray your way through to Psalm 150 during the course of a year.

Intercessory Prayer
We discuss this in Week 5: Supplication on Day 4, in the section "Asking Big for Others." One of the great privileges of prayer is interceding for others before God, just as our Savior continues to do for us today. Intercessory prayer is not limited to praying for an individual. We can intercede for a marriage, family, organization, community, public body, nation...you name it. As you continue in prayer, God will move you to prayer for others. Smile when it happens—you are becoming more like Christ.

Praying in Tongues
A lot of division has happened in the church around the practice of praying in tongues. I believe it is a practice that can honor God in the right circumstances but can be distracting and damaging if not stewarded with maturity and self-control. I agree with Paul (1 Corinthians 13) that speaking in tongues is simply a gift like prophecy, knowledge, or teaching that is meant to be used as a tool to build up the church. It is inferior to the fruit of the spirit, such as love and faith. Like Paul (1 Corinthians 14:1-28), I would urge that in public settings an interpreter must be present; otherwise, the speaker should remain silent.

MY VOICE, HIS HEART

If you feel strongly that speaking in tongues is a gift you have, I would advise you to seek out a church that speaks in tongues as a matter of accepted practice. I would strongly urge against joining a church that does not engage in this practice and attempt to force them to allow your expression in prayer. This will not build up God's church as He calls us to do. I would also encourage joining a church in which ministry leaders guard against counterfeit gifts. Without interpretation, those speaking in tongues have no accountability in the words they are speaking over the church corporately.

One final word I would gently share with you on this important topic. If you are ever praying for another person, in person, please do not pray in tongues. Not only can this be frightening for the recipient, but they will not be edified or encouraged by being able to understand what God has led you to pray for them. We never want to risk making a person feel uncomfortable when they have asked for prayer. Let us guard our hearts in prayer and never seek to build ourselves up when we are in the presence of others. Our goal is to draw near to God and wrap the recipient in Jesus' love.

APPENDIX

ENDNOTES

Week 1

1. Based on Ephesians 3:19; Psalm 36:5-7; Acts 11:23; Titus 2:11-12; James 4:8
2. Matthew 28:16
3. Hebrews 11:6
4. Hebrews 13:21
5. Based on Isaiah 30:21
6. Based on Ecclesiastes 3:1-8; Daniel 4:35; Jeremiah 29:11
7. Based on Psalm 143:8; Psalm 91:14-16
8. Based on Psalm 118:24; John 1:12; Psalm 18:19
9. Based on Deuteronomy 31:6; Jeremiah 32:38
10. Based on Psalm 119:73; Psalm 100:3; 2 Corinthians 3:5
11. Based on Psalm 7:17; Psalm 46
12. Based on John 1:3; Colossians 1:16
13. Luke 22:42
14. John 17:26

Week 2

1. Based on Psalm 146; Revelation 1:8; Isaiah 40:28-29; Exodus 17:15; Psalm 18:2
2. Based on Deuteronomy 33:26-28
3. Based on Genesis 2:7; Acts 17:26; Psalm 18:30; Isaiah 41:10
4. Matthew 1:23
5. Romans 8:17
6. Based on Psalm 18:30-32; Philippians 4:6-7
7. New International Version, 2011 edition
8. Based on James 4:8; Psalm 33:22; Psalm 51:7
9. Based on Hebrews 4:16; Psalm 23; Deuteronomy 31:6; Ephesians 5:27
10. Matthew 6:7
11. Based on Psalm 17:8; Hebrews 4:12; Psalm 23:6
12. Based on John 16:33; John 14:27; Matthew 7:11; Philippians 4:6-7
13. Acts 2:1-47
14. Romans 8:11
15. 1 Chronicles 29:17 NIV

16	Romans 1:20
17	Matthew 21:9
18	Luke 19:40
19	Based on James 1:17; Psalm 90:2; 1 Samuel 2:2; Luke 6:48; Ephesians 2:18

Week 3

1	Based on John 1:14; John 14:6-7; John 15:26
2	Jeremiah 17:9
3	Hebrews 4:12
4	Philippians 2:13
5	Based on Psalm 136
6	Based on Psalm 86:1-11
7	Isaiah 55:11
8	Romans 6:23
9	Based on Psalm 18:16-17; Revelation 12:10; Psalm 103:4-5; Isaiah 9:6; Isaiah 35:6; Psalm 19:1; Romans 1:20; John 3:16; John 14:15-17; Micah 7:19; Psalm 139:24
10	Based on Proverbs 4:18; Matthew 6:22; John 14:6
11	John 8:44
12	Luke 4:41; Matthew 8:29
13	Psalm 19:14
14	Psalm 119:105
15	Based on Psalm 119:105; John 8:12; 2 Corinthians 4:6; 1 Thessalonians 5:5
16	Based on Revelation 19:11; Matthew 10:30; Psalm 139:17-18; Galatians 5:22
17	1 Corinthians 13:1-13; Ephesians 5:2
18	Ephesians 3:18
19	Romans 8:37-39
20	Psalm 139:6 NLT
21	Matthew 26:53-54
22	Based on James 1:5; Proverbs 3:6-7; 2 Samuel 22:20
23	Based on Ephesians 2:8-9; Romans 12:2; Acts 1:8
24	1 Corinthians 13:1
25	Acts 3:19

APPENDIX

Week 4

1. Based on Romans 10:13; Ephesians 3:9; Acts 4:2
2. James 1:2
3. Isaiah 61:3
4. Romans 8:28
5. Based on Genesis 16:13; John 10:18
6. Based on Psalm 40:5; Psalm 139:17-18; Psalm 33:18; 1 Corinthians 13:12
7. Encyclopedia.com
8. lexico.com; Oxford English Dictionary
9. Based on Psalm 123:1; Psalm 90
10. Based on Psalm 23; Genesis 15:1
11. Malachi 3:17
12. Matthew 6:21
13. Based on Psalm 34:7; Jeremiah 31:3; Psalm 10:17-18
14. Based on Matthew 5:45; Psalm 19:1-2; Psalm 25:4-5; Psalm 34:7
15. Romans 8:15
16. 2 Corinthians 9:10-11
17. Matthew 10:8
18. Acts 20:35
19. Luke 6:38
20. Hebrew 11:13
21. Based on Revelation 1:4; 2 Corinthians 9:8
22. Based on Isaiah 51:3
23. 1 Thessalonians 5:18
24. Romans 8:28
25. Psalm 107:1
26. The Pharaoh refused to let God's people go from slavery and bondage so God sent 10 plagues. The last plague God sent was the plague of death. The only way to pass through this curse of death unharmed was to kill a lamb without stain or blemish and put its blood over the doorposts of the family's dwelling place (see Exodus 12).
27. After their deliverance from Egypt, God provided for the Passover Meal to be celebrated every year. There are four cups in Passover. Depending on which Jewish documents are referenced, some recognize the first cup as the cup of Thanksgiving while others recognize it as the final cup.
28. Luke 22:20
29. 1 Corinthians 10:16
30. Based on Psalm 100:4

MY VOICE, HIS HEART

Week 5

1. Based on 1 Chronicles 17:20; Psalm 51:10
2. Matthew 6:25-31
3. Colossians 1:16
4. Ephesians 3:20
5. Based on Ephesians 3:20; Psalm 37:4
6. Based on Psalm 119:105; James 4:8
7. Based on Psalm 51
8. 1 Samuel 13:14
9. Matthew 5:33-37
10. Philippians 4:8
11. Romans 7:9
12. Romans 7:15-25
13. John 1:14
14. Genesis 3; Job chapters 1 and 2 ; Matthew 4; Luke 4
15. John 17:20-23
16. 1 John 14:14-15
17. Ephesians 6:17
18. Hebrews 4:12
19. Ephesians 6:12
20. Based on Psalm 84:11; Psalm 71:5
21. Jeremiah 29:11
22. Hebrews 13:20a &21
23. Based on Psalm 30:11-12
24. Philippians 2:13, Hohman Christian Standard Version
25. Hohman Christian Standard Version
26. Galatians 4:6-7
27. Based on Romans 8:31-39

Week 6

1. Based on 2 Corinthians 12:9-10
2. Matthew 20:16
3. Luke 9:48
4. Matthew 16:25
5. Matthew 11:15, 13:9, 13:43; Mark 4:9; Luke 8:8, 14:35
6. Romans 8:5-6

APPENDIX

7	Proverbs 1:5a
8	Ecclesiastes 3:7b
9	Taken from Psalm 145.
10	Based on Exodus 34:6; Psalm 145:14
11	Genesis 22:1; Genesis 31:11; Exodus 3:4
12	1 Samuel 3:10
13	Isaiah 6:8
14	1 Kings 8:39; Isaiah 57:15; Ephesians 3:17
15	1 Corinthians 2:16
16	2 Corinthians 10:5b
17	Psalm 46:10
18	Galatians 5:22-23
19	Psalm 62:11-12a
20	Based on Psalm 34:15-18
21	Luke 10:20
22	Deuteronomy 31:6 & 8
23	John 14:1-2
24	Based on Psalm 100; James 1:17; Ezekiel 11:19
25	Based on John 8:12; Ephesians 5:8; 1 Thessalonians 5:5
26	John 8:12
27	Psalm 34:5a
28	Psalm 16:11
29	Isaiah 42:16
30	Based on Psalm 73:26; Isaiah 43

CONNECTING TO PRAYER GROUPS IN THE US & GLOBALLY

There are wonderful groups and organizations looking for people to join them in prayer. Your church likely has a prayer team that meets weekly. If it doesn't, you can start one. Some of my most wonderful memories in prayer are from weekly prayer gatherings with prayer warriors in my church. They showed this girl a lot of grace as I was learning and getting comfortable praying out loud in groups. The following is a list of wonderful organizations who would love to send you a prayer guide or have you join them on a prayer call.

- Harvest Prayer Ministries: www.harvestprayer.com – includes weekly and monthly prayer guides as well as PrayerU which offers online prayer courses.

- National Day of Prayer: www.nationaldayofprayer.org/prayer-calls
  National Prayer Shield—AM & PM prayer calls
  "PRAY FOR AMERICA" first Thursday of every month
  Saturday: Prayer for families; Sunday: Prayer for Churches

- Prison Prayer Fellowship: www.prisonfellowship.org/groups/prayer-team/

- World Prays: www.worldprays.org – To equip churches in every nation in 24/7 prayer for a global awakening.

- America Prays: www.americaprays.org/ - 24/7 prayer connecting churches across the US for national awakening.

- Congressional Prayer Caucus Foundation: www.cpcfoundation.com/ - Prayer for national leadership and the upholding of faith in America.

- David's Tent Washington DC: www.davidstentdc.org/ - Invites groups from around the US to come to DC to pray, worship, and intercede for the nation.

- United in Love 40 Days of Love Prayer Campaign: www.40Daysoflove.net - Equipping 100 million Christ-followers around the world to pray for, love on, and share the Gospel of Jesus Christ with at least 10 people in their sphere of influence.

APPENDIX

- Two or Three Prayer Alliance: www.2o3all.org - Focused on workplace and marketplace prayer.

- Moms In Prayer International: www.momsinprayer.org – Offers prayer groups and prayer resources to connect and equip moms to pray together for their children and schools.

- Let's Pray Today Ministries: www.letspraytoday.com - Making prayer part of every life, everyday! Downloadable prayer resources to teach women to pray.

FAVORITE BOOKS ON PRAYER

What Happens When Woman Pray by Evelyn Christenson

Lord, Teach Me to Pray in 28 Days by Kay Arthur

Handbook to Prayer: Praying Scripture Back to God by Kenneth Boa

How to Develop a Powerful Prayer Life: The Biblical Path to Holiness and Relationship with God by Dr. Gregory R. Frizzell

The Doctrine of Prayer by T.W. Hunt

Love to Pray: A 40 Day Devotional for Deepening Your Prayer Life by Alvin VanderGriend

Psalm 91: God's Shield of Protection, Military Edition by Peggy Ruth and Angelia Schum

Prayer That Works by Jill Briscoe

Answers to Prayer by George Muller

Praying Successfully by Charles Spurgeon

Spurgeon on the Holy Spirit by Charles Spurgeon

The Daniel Prayer by Anne Graham Lotz

The Valley of Vision: A Collection of Puritan Prayers & Devotions by Arthur Bennett

100 Amazing Answers to Prayer by Randy Petersen & William J. Peterson

ACKNOWLEDGEMENTS

Thank you to Susie Roberts who first called and asked me to write this study for the women at First Baptist Church of Universal City. I would have never considered this on my own.

Thank you to my wonderful Board of Directors who approved the time and funds it would require. Thank you to the Bineham Foundation for your generous help in funding. Thank you to Bill Krause and Eagle Christian Church for giving me the perfect room with a view when I needed a quiet place to write. God bless you, Teresa Lynn, for your patient editing. Special thanks to Suzi Kramer who stepped in with gifted graphic design work to finish everything in beautiful style.

To the First Lady of Love, my amazing radio co-host Evelyn Davison who kept me writing and producing, even when I had to stumble my way through—your love and joy is infectious. Thank you to the finest friends a girl could have, Lisa, Sylvia, Kerri, Marlene, B.K., and priceless others. Your prayers, support, and time spent editing and making suggestions kept me going when I was ready to stop.

Huge thanks and big love to my mom who pushed me to finish and helped me with appendix materials when my words were running out; and to my steadfast husband and sweet girls, who planned on a six-month writing project and ended up doing without a full-time mom for over twelve instead.

Your hearts and voices make mine stronger,

Cathy

APPENDIX

OTHER RESOURCES FROM CATHY ENDEBROCK

PRAYER CDS AND MP3 AUDIO DOWNLOADS

Prayer for Beginners : Praying for My Husband & Marriage :
Praying for My Children : Praying to Overcome Anxiety & Depression :
Praying for My Prodigal

Turn your greatest challenge into your greatest joy. Learn to pray for your husband and marriage, your children, your worry and fear issues, your rebellious family members, and your personal relationship with God. Download any CD in the series for free. Your audio prayer coach will lead you through daily instruction and prayers that require only 10 minutes each day. Access them all at www.letspraytoday.com.

LISTEN TO CATHY ON LOVE TALK RADIO

Tune in every Saturday at 10:00 a.m. CST, live stream at thebridgeaustin.com, or visit program archives at lovetalknetwork.com. Love Talk Radio airs on KTXW 101.1FM & 1120AM The Bridge Austin, Today's Central Texas Christian Talk.

Love Talk Radio keeps dialogue focused and simple while sharing life-changing, biblical principles for daily living. Cathy Endebrock, Love Talk co-producer and co-host, presses into key issues with the unity and love of Christ, tackling the challenges facing America in a post-Christian culture, and inspiring listening friends to love walk and love talk right where God has them.

www.ingramcontent.com/pod-product-compliance
Lightning Source LLC
Chambersburg PA
CBHW051802100526
44592CB00016B/2535